Message from the Director

The Federal Law Enforcement Training Center (FLETC) is pleased to present the "Survival Scores Research Project" as part of our continuing effort to develop and provide new information and strategies to enhance law enforcement training. Additionally, the FLETC is committed to sharing this information with the law enforcement community. The dramatic impact of stress on performance is well recognized in the law enforcement profession, but has not been well documented from a research perspective. This latest research will enhance the growing pool of knowledge in this area, and aid in identifying training mechanisms to optimize the effectiveness of law enforcement officers' responses in stressful encounters.

This research-based project offers a new perspective on the future of law enforcement training. This novel approach combines the numerous disciplines that are integrated in the law enforcement profession and applies them in a highly stressful environment. The first hand documentation of the stress response provided new and insightful information that can be directly applied to our training programs. I would like to thank our distinguished research colleagues from the University of South Florida and Walter Reed Army Institute of Research for their valuable insight and assistance in performing this research. I would also like to thank our partner organizations at the FLETC who provided support and students for this project. The FLETC remains dedicated to exploring new technologies and evaluating training practices as we continue to focus on our responsibility of preparing law enforcement officers to meet their ever-evolving responsibilities.

Survival Scores Research Project

FLETC Research Paper

April 2004

Table of Contents

Research Abstract

The Survival Scores Research Project report concludes two years of research in which the research team developed, tested, and analyzed data comparing performance in a stressful law enforcement scenario to physiological and psychological measures. This research was conducted with oversight and approval of the Walter Reed Army Institute of Research Human Factors Research Review Board.

A high-stress law enforcement scenario served as the basis for testing student performance. Basic training students from both the Criminal Investigator Training Program (CI) and Mixed Basic Police Training Program (MBPTP) were used. Testing was done just prior to student graduation from training. The students were subjected to repeated measures for both State and Trait Personality indicators for psychological assessments. The physiological indicators of heart rate, blood pressure, and cortisol were also monitored for comparison to 97 law enforcement skills performed and assessed in a stressful scenario. Background demographics to include a wide variety of experiences and training were collected, as were basic training scores for comparison. The data set thus included 368 variables available for analysis and comparison.

The scenario was developed by subject matter experts, with the purpose of invoking maximum stress in a law enforcement situation. The scenario was captured entirely on film for later analysis and scoring. The scenario was analyzed as seven separate events that represent transition points in the level of stress invoked.

The results of the research have provided a strong correlation between stress and performance. As stress increased, heart rate, blood pressure and cortisol levels increased. As expected, performance decreased. Serious performance deficiencies were identified. Impacts on cognitive decision-making are likewise reported with specific observations.

Recommendations include methods to enhance or revise training methodologies and the continuation of research to more narrowly define potential development of a survival score index.

Principal Authors and Points of Contact at the Federal Law Enforcement Training Center for this report are:

Valerie J. Atkins, M.S.
Branch Chief
Centers and Agency Programs
Firearms Division
912-267-2833

William A. Norris, Ph.D.
Branch Chief/Exercise Physiologist
Research and Curriculum Development
Research and Evaluation Division
912-267-2255

Forward

During the past two years, it has been my pleasure to work with colleagues at the Federal Law Enforcement Training Center on the Survival Score Research Project. This unique study has focused on the psychological and physiological reactions to highly stressful situations that are likely to be encountered by law enforcement officers in the performance of their duties. Based on my experience in psychological research on stress and emotions over the past forty years, I consider the Survival Score Project to be exceptionally important in evaluating the reactions of well-trained persons to highly stressful situations. A similar study would be extremely difficult to conduct in more traditional research settings, and unlikely to address the special requirements of police officers.

The findings of the Survival Score Research Project have important implications for the training of law enforcement officers to deal with highly stressful situations, and also make a significant contribution to the research literature on the effects of high levels of stress on performance. The FLETC staff who have worked on this project have demonstrated outstanding ability, and are strongly committed to carrying out the demanding requirements of a complex research program.

The findings of the Survival Score Project also demonstrate the importance of determining how those individuals who volunteered to participate in this highly stressful study compared with the general population of FLETC trainees from which they were selected. The fact that the participating volunteers were lower in their disposition to experience anxiety and anger in responding to highly stressful situations than the total population of FLETC trainees indicates that the adverse effects of the stressful situations on the performance of a more representative sample of FLETC trainees would probably be greater than those observed for the volunteer participants.

Given the important contributions of the Survival Score Research Project to the effective training of law enforcement officers who are often required to respond to situations characterized by unpredictable dangers, it would be highly desirable for FLETC to support the continuation of this unique project, and to include additional stressful scenarios that are closely related to the stressful circumstances that are likely to be encountered by law enforcement officers. The findings of this research project not only have the potential to improve the training of law enforcement officers for dealing with the crises and emergencies encountered in high-speed pursuit and handling fire arms under stressful circumstances, but also to protect them from the consequences of performance failures that could lead to serious injury or death.

Charles D. Spielberger, Ph.D., ABPP, Distinguished Research Professor
Director, Center for Research in Behavioral Medicine and Health Psychology
University of South Florida, Psychology Department, PCD 4118G
4202 East Fowler Avenue, Tampa, FL 33620

Forward

I feel extremely fortunate to have had the opportunity to work on the Survival Score project with colleagues and staff at the Federal Law Enforcement Training Center. The law enforcement officer carries awesome responsibility. While entrusted with the protection of some of the most vulnerable members of society, they sometimes must deal with the most dangerous individuals and situations. Accurate assessments and judgments must be made and correct actions taken in fractions of a second. A wrong or late decision can have terrible and permanent consequences. Accordingly, the job can be extremely stressful for the officers.

FLETC leadership is to be congratulated in having had the vision to initiate a research program aimed at evaluating the degree to which the training program prepares graduates to perform under realistically stressful conditions. The extremely well-designed scenario, the exceptional capabilities and professional experience of the FLETC staff and their ability to work so well with an interdisciplinary group of scientists from outside of the law enforcement community, have rendered this a truly unique and highly successful research effort. I can imagine no other organization capable of doing such research with equal realism, scientific rigor and relevance to the law enforcement professional.

I think it would be extremely important to continue this research. Several new dimensions should be explored. Officers are in frequent contact via radio, providing an opportunity for spectral analysis of speech for developing reliable indices of stress and predictors of performance decrements. We have clearly established that the scenario is highly stressful and that serious, potentially life-threatening shortcomings in performance are elicited. In addition to suggesting to staff potential changes that might be made in training, it appears that the individual students get valuable feedback about their own capabilities and areas where more study or practice might be beneficial. Accordingly, one might consider offering students an opportunity to participate in such a scenario after the midpoint of their training. A second scenario participation at the end of training, would then demonstrate whether the earlier experience enhanced final performance levels. Clearly, this project has the capability to identify training innovations, which will increase the survivability of the law enforcement officer.

I hope to continue our very promising research project and will be happy to provide neuroendocrine support, data interpretation and scientific editing where requested. Finally, I will be pleased to assist with making any necessary modifications in the protocol and to continue representing the research group to the WRAIR Institutional Review Board.

James L. Meyerhoff, M.D.
Chief, Department of Neurochemistry and Neuroendrocrinology
Division of Neurosciences
Walter Reed Army Institute of Research (WRAIR)
Walter Reed, Washington, D.C. 20307

Officer Survival: Responding Under Stress

Introduction

Law enforcement officers serve the public by performing a broad range of activities that range from passive surveillance and investigative work to the dynamic arrest situations that can quickly become violent and life threatening. Our justice system permits the use of force only when necessary, and limits its use to specifically defined situations. Thus, an officer's survival depends upon his/her ability to quickly assess a situation and respond with an appropriate level of force. With legal guidelines in place governing the "use of force," it may appear to be a simple process for an officer to determine the appropriate response for a particular situation; but it is not. The decision-making environment for law enforcement officers commonly includes a component that has tremendous impact on the outcome the factor of stress. Critical decisions often have to be made quickly to save a life or prevent further harm. Clear, rational thinking in a life-threatening, time-urgent situation is vital to officer survival. All too often, however, the rational thought process must compete against the rush of adrenaline and a professional desire to apprehend the suspect – sometimes at too high a cost.

Current significance of the problem

The FBI Report for the year 2000 provides some alarming statistics in the area of officer survival:

- The number of law enforcement officers feloniously killed in the line of duty was up 21.4 percent from the previous year's number – 51 officers were slain in 2000, and 42 officers were killed in 1999.

- Slightly more than half (53%) of the felonious shootings took place at a distance of 0-5 feet, and 70% were at 0-10 feet. These close range killings are also representative of the ten-year period for 1991 – 2000.

- Body armor appears to provide minimal protection in close range shooting scenarios, as 29 of the 47 (62%) slain officers wore protective clothing.

Many shooting incidents occur in poorly illuminated environments, at close range, with multiple subjects, sometimes including innocent bystanders. Most such incidents are over in less than three seconds. Many routinely recurring situations have the potential to expose officers to inordinate risks (domestic violence investigations, traffic stops, undercover investigations and arrests). Thus, the law enforcement officer must maintain continuous vigilance, exercise sound judgment, accurately assess threat level, communicate clearly, respond promptly and appropriately, and if threat escalation warrants, rapidly change tactics to include force – if necessary, even lethal force. Our task is to design a test paradigm reflective of the challenge presented by law enforcement duty.

The Federal Law Enforcement Training Center (FLETC) offers several different courses which are utilized by different Federal agencies, including the eight week Mixed Basic Course and the ten week Criminal Investigation Course. Volunteer subjects were used from both of these courses. Accordingly, subjects in this study had completed 8 to 10 weeks of comprehensive training in all required skills and were exposed to all of the potential risks before being offered the opportunity to participate in this research study. A realistic scenario was developed that required the use of skills acquired during training. This study was designed to address the following research questions:

- Can we validate our training scenarios as being realistic/highly stressful? Trainees are asked to perform law enforcement skills in scenarios that replicate real world situations that are stressful. This component will compare the stress response of trainees in this study to the stress response measured in other studies designed to elicit an acute stress response.

- Can specific psychological factors be identified that predict performance in a highly stressful law enforcement encounter?

- Can specific physiological factors be identified that predict performance in a highly stressful law enforcement encounter?

- Can specific physiological factors be used to identify an "optimum stress level for optimum performance" as suggested by various authors?

- What effect does high stress have on decision-making (cognitive processing)?

Once specific factors have been identified and the results of this study discussed with the many trainers and subject matter experts, we will then focus on the second phase of this research endeavor which will attempt to answer the more far-reaching question:

- How can these identified factors be used to improve/modify instruction at FLETC, and thereby, improve performance under stress?

Of significant interest to this research project is the role that psychological stress has on human performance. There is a limited amount of research in this area as few research institutions allow scientists to intentionally expose subjects to high levels of stress, anxiety, and fear. This is, however, the type of training environment we wish to situationally create for our trainees in order to safely replicate dangerous and stressful situations they may experience on the job.

In order to assess the performance of numerous law enforcement skills during a high stress encounter, a scenario was developed that required specific law enforcement skills, abilities, and knowledge during stressful situations.

Section 1 Review of the Literature:
Physiological and Psychological Effects of Stress

Historical Origins of Stress

The emotional reactions of fear (anxiety) and rage (anger) were described by Darwin more than a century ago (1872). Darwin noted that fear and rage vary in intensity, with fear increasing from mild apprehension or surprise to an extreme "agony of terror." Anger and rage are "states of mind" that vary "only in degree, and there is no marked distinction in their characteristic signs." Freud (1924) also believed fear (anxiety) and aggression (anger) are inherent characteristics of human behavior that include physiological and behavioral components. The perceived presence of danger, whether from external sources or one's own repressed thoughts and feelings, evokes an unpleasant emotional state which then serves to warn the individual that some form of adjustment is necessary. In his discussion of the adaptive nature of anxiety, which prompts the individual to avoid or cope more effectively with the danger, Freud's "danger signal" theory is similar in many aspects to Darwin's evolutionary concept. Behavioral theories have clarified the nature of anxiety in terms that are quite similar to the conceptual work of Freud.

Most authorities now regard human emotions as complex psychobiological states characterized by changes throughout the body, particularly those controlled by the autonomic nervous system. It is generally accepted that perception of a particular event will greatly influence an individual's emotional reactions, and that differences in personality and past experience may dispose people to respond to similar stimulus circumstances in radically different ways (Lazarus & Folkman, 1984; Lazarus & Opton, 1966). According to Spielberger (1999):
The quality and intensity of the feelings that characterize emotional states seem to be their most unique and distinctive features. Therefore, the scientific study of emotional phenomena requires the development of appropriate methods to distinguish between qualitatively different emotional states, gauge the intensity of such states at a particular time, and measure individual differences in how often the emotion is experienced by different people.

Defining Stress and Anxiety

Spielberger defined anxiety as an emotional reaction to a stimulus perceived as dangerous. This stimulus or "stressor" results in dysphoric (restless) thoughts and feelings, unpleasant sensations, and physical changes (Hanin, 2000). If a person does not find a stimulus threatening, then changes in anxiety should not result. The same stimulus may be perceived as a beneficial challenge to one individual, threatening to another, and neutral to a third. Any stimulus that an individual perceives as a threat is termed a stressor. A key concept in this definition (and one that is often overlooked) is perception. It is almost always the perception of the stimuli rather than the stimuli itself that determines the stress response. For example, two drivers perform the identical task of driving from point A to point B. Although all conditions are identical (ability, vehicle, route, speed, etc.), one driver "perceives" the drive as stressful and the other driver "perceives" it as boring or even relaxing. We can measure many physiological parameters to document the stress response, but it is the psychological computer (the brain) that determines the nature and degree of the body's responses.

Anxiety and Anger

The term "anxiety state" refers to an unpleasant emotional condition or state that is comparable to the conceptions of fear originally formulated by Darwin and Freud. Anxiety states consist of consciously perceived feelings of tension, apprehension, nervousness, and worry, and associative activation of the autonomic nervous system. These states fluctuate and vary over time as a function of the perceived danger. "Anxiety trait" refers to relatively stable individual differences in anxiety. People who have high trait anxiety are most likely to perceive stressful situations as being personally dangerous or threatening and to respond to such situations with elevations in state anxiety. The stronger the anxiety trait, the more often the individual has experienced state anxiety in the past, and the greater the probability that intense elevations in state anxiety will be experienced in threatening situations in the future (Spielberger et al., 1995).

In order to reduce the ambiguity of the terms anger, hostility, and aggression (Spielberger et al, 1983), developed the following working definitions:

- The concept of anger usually refers to an emotional state that consists of feelings that vary in intensity, from mild irritation or annoyance to intense fury and rage. Although hostility usually involves angry feelings, this concept has the connotation of a complex set of attitudes that motivate aggressive behaviors directed toward destroying objects or injuring other people.... While anger and hostility refer to feelings and attitudes, the concept of aggression generally implies destructive or punitive behavior directed towards other persons or objects. (p. 16)

Acute Stress Versus Chronic Stress

Our study examined the effects of acute stress on performance in simulated law enforcement scenarios. Acute stress can be defined as stress that is "sudden, novel, intense, and of relatively short duration, disrupts goal-oriented behavior, and requires a proximate response" (Salas, 1996). Such acute stress in law enforcement is the result of the decision-maker's response to a threat situation. Salas summarizes the stressful situation as one in which the perception of danger exceeds one's resources to respond.

In contrast to acute stress is chronic stress. The human body, when confronted with any type of stressor does not return to a baseline condition immediately when the stressor is removed. This causes a change in the homeostasis of the person. The change can be short term (acute) or long term (chronic). Chronic stress is manifested when long-term homeostatic changes lead to alterations or breakdowns in any number of body functions. Through repeated exposure to acute stress or low stress situations, an individual can experience chronic stress symptoms. Stress reduction programs are basically designed to minimize the effects of chronic stress.

State/Trait Anxiety —Anger Inventories

Among the many instruments available to evaluate anxiety, the State-Trait Anxiety Inventory (STAI, Spielberger, 1983) is clearly the most frequently used and is generally considered the standard in the field. We will be using the STAI in this project, and are fortunate to have the developer of this instrument, Dr. Spielberger, working with us.

Early Physiological Research

Not only did Darwin and Freud record behavior patterns in response to emotions such as fear and rage, but also physical reactions such as facial expressions (clenched teeth, reddened face) increased heart rate, respiration, muscle tension, and other distinctive signs. Harvard physician-scientist Walter Cannon (1915, 1989) first termed the "fight or flight" response as a result of his research on the emotions of fear and rage in animals. These emotions disrupted the body's stability or balance (which he later termed "homeostasis") and triggered the release of adrenaline. Cannon was the first to suggest that the brain was the controlling center for a two-fold response to an undesirable stimulus, e.g.: the robber is dangerous (interpretation) and run from the robber (reaction & movement). The Canadian physician and endocrinologist, Hans Selye (1936, 1978), described these external pressures with the term "stressors" and the biological response as "stress" during his development of the "General Adaptation Syndrome"

(GAS). His definition of stress as the non-specific response of the body to any demand made upon it is consistent with the research studies of stimulus-response (S-R) psychology. Selye defined GAS as three distinct stages:

- Alarm Reaction: Similar to fight or flight.

- Resistance: Struggle to overcome, hard work, limited rest/sleep.

- Exhaustion: Body systems crash, fatigue, errors, irritability, vulnerable to illness (colds, flu, acne).

Selye's theory was that injury, overload and fear all produce the same body reaction. He believed that both eustress (positive) and distress (negative) produced the same initial response in the body (hence the general adaptation). Although Selye fashioned the term "stress response," many researchers classify Selye's research as actually describing "strain" as opposed to stress. Stress in many disciplines (biology, physics) is an outside or external stimulus acting on an object or individual, whereas strain would more accurately describe the internal reaction of a body or object to that stimulus.

Selye's original work has been extended and modified through ongoing stress-related research. Studies have shown that a fear (anxiety) response may not produce the same physiological response as anger. For example, John Mason (1985) showed unique cardiovascular and endocrine responses specific to a variety of different types of fear and anger stressors. Robert Eliot (1989) used selective measures (e.g. cardiovascular, muscular, gastrointestinal responses) for testing stress to evaluate those prone toward excessive responses to intellectual challenge or routine crises, and to describe individuals who over-react to mild stressors. Eliot characterized these individuals as "hot reactors."

Psychological perception frequently generates strong physiological manifestations. The body has been designed from its primitive origins to be alert to danger and respond if necessary. In this context, the psychological and physiological profiles are equally key and complex. Not only does the brain house the psychological orientation of an individual, but also the command center that directs the manifestations of those desires or emotions. This would certainly be the case with the fight or flight response. This response is reflexive in that it requires no thought or analysis but only the basic motor capacity to attack or flee. The physical display of psychological processes provides researchers with objective indicators for the measurement and analysis of arousal, anxiety, anger, fear, and other emotional processes that often appear subjective.

Neural Response to Stress

The central nervous system (CNS) has the complex task of collecting information, interpreting it, and responding in an appropriate manner. The interpretation of the event by the brain may dictate that no response is necessary (you see exactly what you expected to see) or that a dramatic response is necessary (an oncoming car is in your lane). The manner in which the body responds to a stimulus is determined by the configuration of the CNS (nature) and what information we have stored in it (nurture). It is important to understand how the brain is designed to respond in order to make modifications to the response process should the need arise.

Basic Wiring of the Nervous System

The nervous system is traditionally divided into two general parts based upon their location: the CNS and the peripheral nervous system (PNS). The brain and the spinal cord comprise the CNS and are protected by the skull and the vertebrae of the spinal column. The role of the CNS is to perform two complex functions for the body: 1) transmit to the brain information received from the environment and/or the body (input); and 2) transmit from the brain information to control muscles, glands, vessels, etc. thereby producing movement or bodily adaptations to environment (output). The PNS consists of all nerve fibers that enter or leave the CNS. The PNS essentially provides the lines of communication throughout the body whereas the CNS performs the operations of analysis, coordination, and determination of an appropriate response to the stimulus.

As the focal point of the CNS, the human brain is divided into three major parts: the cerebrum, cerebellum, and brainstem. The cerebrum constitutes the largest segment of the human brain, and is divided into two large sections called hemispheres. The outermost layer of the cerebrum is known as the cerebral cortex and controls three vital functions for the body: 1) collection and interpretation of sensory input, 2) organization of complex motor actions, and 3) decision making, memory, rational and moral thought. The basal ganglia are neuron cell bodies located deep within the cerebrum. This area serves as the relay station for motor nerve signals and is a production site for neurotransmitters.

The cerebellum communicates with the CNS through three major nerve tracts and serves to monitor and coordinate complex patterns of motor activity. Sensory input on body position and posture is received and corrections made to provide fluid, accurate movements. At the base of the cerebrum is a complex region of nerve tracts and nuclei (gray matter) termed the brain stem. This combination of structures links the spinal cord to the higher brain areas previously discussed. The brain stem is comprised of numerous structures including the optic nerve tracts, pons, pineal gland, thalamus, and hypothalamus. The thalamus serves as a primary relay station for all senses except for smell, and channels the sensory information to the cortex for analysis. The hypothalamus, though smaller in size than the thalamus, plays one of the primary roles in regulating homeostasis through its control of several body functions and serves as a key link between the nervous and endocrine systems. Some of the more prominent actions of the hypothalamus are:

1. Regulation of heart rate and arterial blood pressure.

2. Regulation of body temperature.

3. Regulation of water and electrolyte balance.

4. Regulation of sleep and wakefulness.

5. Control hunger and regulation of body weight.

6. Control of movements and secretions in the digestive system.

7. Production of hormones that stimulate the pituitary (the "master" gland) affecting growth, other endocrine glands, reproductive glands.

Since many body functions that are modified by the stress response are the very functions that were just identified as being under the direct or indirect control of the thalamus and hypothalamus, it is clear that the brain stem plays a dominant role in the body's stress response.

Although the anatomical areas of the CNS are relatively easy to identify by their location and function, it is vital to recognize that all CNS regions are linked to other specific areas and regions. Typically, a neural response is the compilation and integration of numerous neural regions. The response to a highly stressful event is generally the blend of one or more CNS areas (previously mentioned) that interact with other systems and organs throughout the body. Another method of discussing the operation of the CNS is by comparing the type of challenges (input)

ACTIVATION OF THE STRESS RESPONSE

Stimulation of Senory Receptor(s) (External)
(Visual, Auditory, Tactile, Olfactory, Gustatory)

Reticular Activating System
(*Internal* Activation)
BRAIN

Cortex   Limbic

Cognitive   Emotional
Interpretation   Arousal

Integration

Perception of a Threat

Posterior   Anterior
Hypothalamus ← Hypothalamus → Thalamus

Thoracolumbar   Craniosacral

Spinal Cord   Spinal Cord

Sympathetic   Parasympathetic
Activation   Activation
of End Organ   of End Organ

PNS

CNS

PNS

to the type or level of response required by the CNS. This pattern of operation or analysis is frequently identified as a system. With regards to the stress response, two of the most prominent systems in the CNS are the limbic system and the reticular activation system.

The limbic system includes the hypothalamus, thalamus, hippocampus, septum, and amygdala structures. These structures center around the diencephalon and commonly include the pituitary gland. The limbic system is involved in the process of emotional expression and to a limited extent, arousal. The limbic system modifies the emotions of anger, fear, pleasure, and sorrow. It is through the perception of a threat to the well-being or homeostasis of the body that the CNS triggers a "fight-or-flight" response in an attempt to increase the body's likelihood of survival. The reticular formation extends from the brain stem to the diencephalon region. Although this lower portion of the brain typically deals with basic reflex and basal body functions, this system monitors passage of emotional stimuli to the cortex. The collective innervation of key areas including the cortex is known as the reticular activating system (RAS). The term "arousal" is associated with the RAS and is synonymous with other terms such as anxious, tense, or even "psyched-up." Only specific stimuli are allowed to pass through the RAS to activate cortical (and sub-cortical) areas for an appropriate response. For example, the average individual upon hearing gunshots nearby would duck or run for the closest cover. If, however, that same individual is a firearms instructor, the sound of shooting may produce virtually no noticeable reaction due to the reticular formation filtering out stimuli and not activating numerous systems throughout the body. At bedtime, this filtering process can be elevated (sleeping through a storm) or on selective "standby" such as a parent being able to sleep but still capable of hearing a child down the hall call for them when they are sick.

Neural Regulation of the Cardiovascular System

The autonomic nervous system subconsciously controls basic functions of the body such as heart rate, blood pressure, respiration, metabolism, digestion, and endocrine balance. These controls take place without conscious effort and most of these functions are amplified through emotional factors. As mentioned previously, most organs receive dual innervation from both the sympathetic and parasympathetic branches of the autonomic nervous system. In times of stress, it is the autonomic system that prepares the body to meet the demands that may be placed upon it.

The rate and manner in which the heart beats provides meaningful information as to how the central nervous system (CNS) reacts to a stressor. Combined with heart rate (HR) are the cardiovascular components of systolic blood pressure (SBP) and diastolic blood pressure (DBP). Numerous studies have examined the relationship between a high degree of cardiovascular reactivity to stress and premature development of coronary artery disease. The extent of this relationship of HR, SBP, and DBP response to stress has been well documented and summarized in Sherwood and Turner, (1992). Friedman and Rosenman (1959) identified specific behavior patterns (Type A & B personality types) and indicated that the individual with the type A characteristics of hostility, time urgency, and high competitiveness comprise a risk factor for coronary heart disease (CHD). It is well documented that the psychological perspective of the individual (i.e. psychological trait; personality type A/B) plays a critical role in how a challenging event is perceived by the complex CNS and responded to by that individual. Numerous studies have compared these psychological profiles to the intensity and longevity of the reaction and recovery to a stressor.

Stress Related Hormones

The hypothalamus serves as the activation center of the brain that controls the various body systems associated with fight or flight. Although the nervous system and the endocrine system work in tandem during the stress response, they are quite dissimilar in how they function. The nervous system is very precise in activating specific tissues during a perceived threat and most structures receive direct innervation by way of the sympathetic and parasympathetic pathways. In contrast, the endocrine system secretes hormones into the circulation and their unique chemical structure allows them to activate the intended target structure and leave other structures essentially unaffected. Although direct neural stimulation can activate a structure instantaneously, the effect quickly wanes due to the depletion of the neurotransmitter. The body's chemical messengers, hormones, continue the sustained activation of the tissues (see chart). Adrenaline and noradrenaline are produced by the adrenal medulla (atop the kidneys) and produce effects similar to those of the sympathetic nervous system. The cortex of the adrenal glands produces aldosterone and cortisol. Cortisol promotes increases in the concentration of blood amino acids, release of fatty acids, and formation of glucose from non-carbohydrate sources. These hormones are released into the bloodstream as part of the normal response to exertion or psychological stress. Because of its role in regulating blood glucose levels, cortisol is referred to as a "gluco-corticoid" to distinguish it from other adrenal cortical steroids. Through this multi-dimensional process, the sympathetic nervous system activates numerous body systems (both neural and hormonal) in preparation for fight or flight, while cortisol supplies the cells with amino acids and additional energy that may be required during times of stress. Cortisol also plays a key role in the maintenance of an adequate blood pressure during times of stress in order to avoid collapse. Cortisol can be measured in blood or in saliva.

In order to maintain a smooth flow of action in the research scenario and to avoid psychological stress relating to venipuncture, cortisol measures were obtained through salivary analysis. The Research Group was fortunate to work jointly with James Meyerhoff, MD, Chief, Department of Neurendocrinology at Walter Reed Army Institute of Research. Dr. Meyerhoff has used the salivary cortisol procedure in numerous stress-related research endeavors (J. L. Meyerhoff et al., 1990, 1998, 2000).

Stress and Decision-Making

Not only is the brain involved in the emotional perception of stress, but it also provides the vital services of thought, analysis, decision making. The ability to make decisions (and to make those decisions under stress) is a critical skill for law enforcement officers. Officers must routinely face acutely stressful situations and make decisions that can ultimately determine life or death. Unfortunately, "emotional" stress responses often compete with "rational" decision-making process to create a quandary for the brain with regard to actions and desired outcomes. Rational decision making attempts to methodically examine options and then select or perform the best one. The stress response is more time urgent by nature, and focuses on preparing the body to "fight or flee" with little concern for rational thought.

Decision-making is the process of identifying the alternative actions, weighing the potential benefits, and selecting the option with the greatest potential for a positive outcome (Salas, 1996). Most decisions are based on life experiences, and how they fit into what we know. Pierce Howard cites an example of the typical "image" drawn in the mind of people hearing the statement; "The doctor's son greeted his father." The image typically created is one of a son meeting and greeting his father, when in fact, the doctor could be his mother. Our life experiences cause us to see things and make them fit into what we already know. Most learning appears to be a process of fitting newly received information into one of our old memories.

The decision-maker will tend to immediately classify a situation, clarify the goals, determine what is likely to happen next, and what courses of action are typical for the situation. This process is usually instantaneous and is not consciously deliberated. The decision-maker with experience in this situation will classify it as familiar, and will react less to stressors and have a higher expectation of the outcome.

In his book Stress and Human Performance, Salas identifies various types of decision-making. First, there is analytical decision making (rarely used in stressful situations), where options are weighed and outcomes evaluated. Second, there is diagnostic decision making which occurs when the decision-maker cannot quickly classify a situation based on life experiences. In these situations, the effects of stress become involved in the decision-making process. When subjected to stress, the decision-maker adapts by resorting to simpler decision strategies and a perceptual narrowing.

A simple model of performance (or behavior) includes input, decision-making, and output. Input includes all stimuli that affect an individual at any one time. This includes relevant stimuli (those that are important) and

NEURAL AND ENDOCRINE ACTIVATION
TO A STRESSFUL STIMULUS

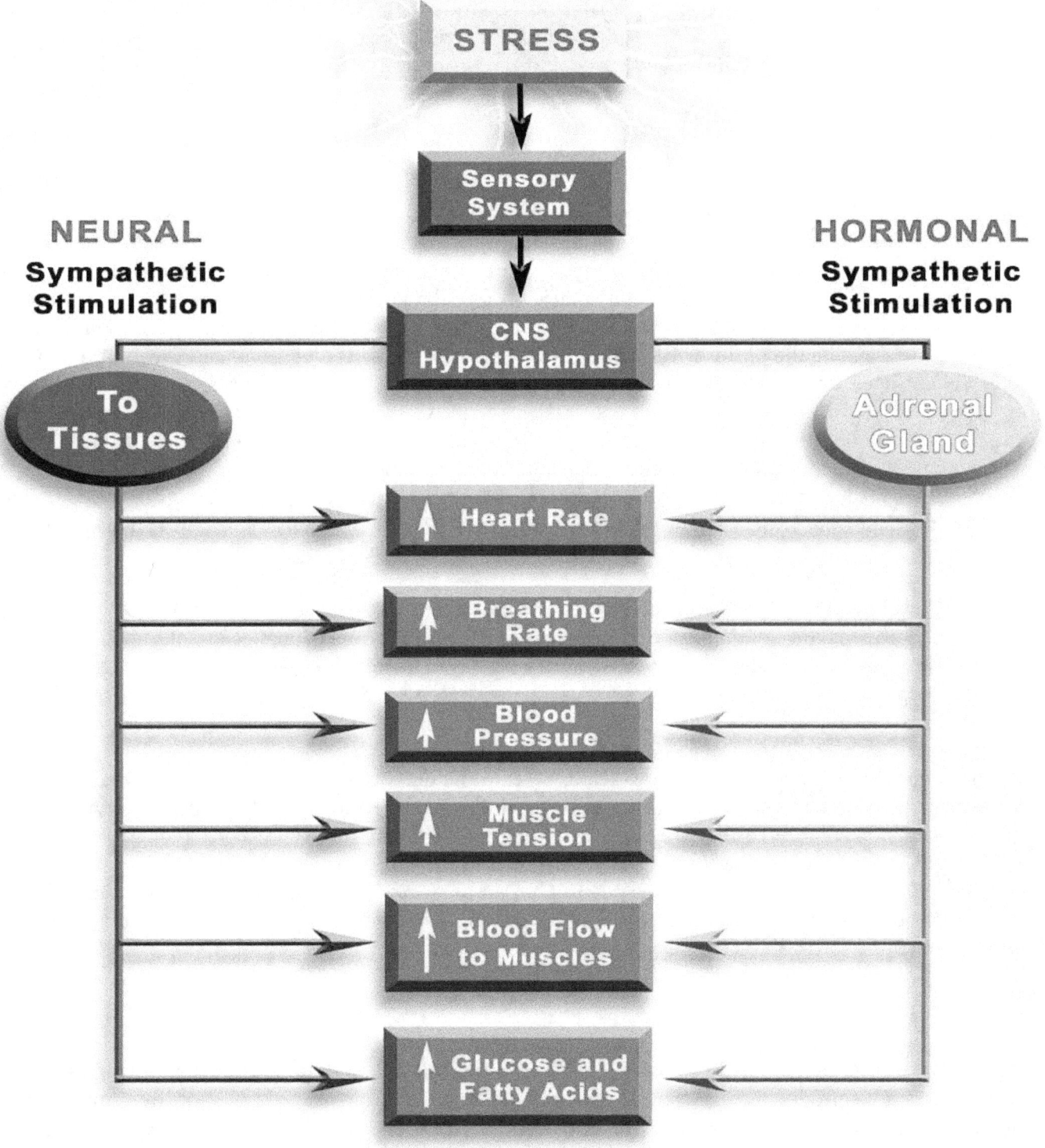

irrelevant (stimuli that have no significance). Decision-making describes the process of interpreting and integrating input and selecting appropriate responses. Output is the response, behavior, or performance. Feedback refers to the information that is provided during or after the performance. Feedback can be isolated to the specific action itself (such as firing a weapon and receiving visual, auditory, olfactory, proprioceptive stimuli, etc.) or after the performance (from partners, bystanders, forensics, etc.). The output is typically the culmination of numerous processing (decision making) steps by the CNS. (Salas, 1996)

The analysis of incoming information (sensory input) can range from the simple analysis of one sensory modality (is the room too warm?), to a complex analysis of many forms of sensory input integrated with memory and higher brain analysis. In this second, more complex situation involving the performance of critical skills (such as making a vehicle stop), the brain is constantly receiving, analyzing, and integrating multiple streams of data second by second in order to make appropriate decisions. As the communication center for the body, the CNS performs the complex process of decision making with split-second speed and sends out a fusillade of commands to multiple body sites for appropriate responses.

Hypervigilance

Stressors increase the likelihood that decision-makers will choose the first option they consider. While this does not necessarily result in poor decision-making, it certainly increases the probability that the decision-making process will be less than optimal. Once again, the amount of experience the decision-maker has directly affects the consequences of the decision. Johnston and colleagues found that decision-making does not necessarily suffer when the decision-maker is under stress. In a research project involving computer simulations of combat missions, they sought to differentiate the performances of military personnel making decisions under conditions of vigilant and hypervigilant decision-making. The term vigilant decision making refers to decisions made in an organized fashion with consideration of all the alternatives, whereas hypervigilant decision-making occurs under a sudden or unexpected threat or time pressure where limited alternatives are considered due to heightened perceptual narrowing. Hypervigilance is the term often used to characterize someone in a state of panic. In Johnson's study, the stressors of task load, auditory distraction, and time pressure were added to force hypervigilant decision-making. The findings indicated that hypervigilant decision-making resulted in more effective performance than vigilant decision-making.

These results, however, are not fully supported by other research in this area. Janis and Mann (1977) characterized hypervigilant decision making as "impulsive and disorganized" where the decision maker tends to "search frantically for a solution, [consider] a limited number of alternatives, and then latch onto a hastily contrived solution." They did agree that hypervigilant training more closely duplicates real-world situations, and promotes the learning of adaptive behaviors.

Since the perception and assessment of a threat are crucial to the decision-making process, it is vital to understand how the decision-maker views the threat. If a situation is familiar and the individual has successfully handled similar situations, the threat may be perceived as a challenge rather than a threat. In order to differentiate between a threat and a challenge, "Individuals evaluate an event as threatening when the perceived danger exceeds the capacity to respond." Thus, threat appraisals focus on the potential harm of an event and are associated with primarily negative emotional reactions. Individuals evaluate an event as challenging when they perceive the possibility for gain to outweigh the potential for harm." (Salas, 1996)

Section 1: Summary

Numerous factors affect performance under stress. Due to the broad nature of the concept of "stress," this study will focus on situations producing acute stress, which is sudden, novel, intense, and of short duration. Acute stress conditions replicate many law enforcement situations that involve the critical components of decision-making and use of force. Rational, appropriate, and well-trained responses that are stored in memory can be compromised and overruled by the emotional, survival-oriented instincts of the brain. Through the identification of factors that have a positive or negative influence on performance under stress, it is hoped that this knowledge can be used to improve the capabilities and safety of law enforcement officers

Section 2: Review of the Literature: Training

Training The Law Enforcement Officer To Perform Under Stress.

As law enforcement trainers, our ultimate goal is to prepare the law enforcement trainee to effectively handle the vastly varied demands of the occupation. Duties in any given hour can vary from the intense analytical diligence of the investigator to a state of heightened alert and readiness. Of course, the duties may also require the law enforcement officer to transition from a period of calm routine to quick decisive reaction within seconds. There is evidence that such transitions are problematic. For instance, a Department of Justice report on 40 attempted shootings of officers found that victim officers returning fire averaged a hit on their target 41% of the time, while the offenders achieved a 91% hit rate. Of course, each of these officers was reacting to being shot at (the majority were actually shot), and under severe stress (In the Line of Fire: Violence Against Law Enforcement, Anthony J. Pinizzotto, Ph.D., Edward F. Davis, Charles E. Miller III. US Dept of Justice, FBI, National Institute of Justice Report, Oct. 1997). Preparing individuals for such moments is among the challenges law enforcement trainers face.

Experiential training is predicated on the assumption that the student learns from the experience. We provide experiences and information in training that prepare students to deal with the incredibly complex skills they will need in order to perform their jobs. Knowledge of laws, the ability to apply that knowledge, investigative skills, people skills, writing skills, critical thinking, physical fitness, and the ability to instantly react to critical, even life threatening situations with quick actions and appropriate responses are expected of each law enforcement officer. Such a vast array of skills certainly requires a level of maturity. And these job requirements certainly require training that provides officers the proverbial "tool box" of appropriate and effective actions and responses they may need to perform their duties. This ideal is more easily achieved in areas involving strictly cognitive performance requirements, where the students have time to reflect on their teachings, review their options, and select appropriate courses of action. Indeed, this typically comprises the great majority of their duties and responsibilities as law enforcement officers. Much more problematic is effective training for the tiny fraction of officers' duties and responsibilities that may involve life-threatening actions and immediate responses appropriate to the situation. Preparing officers to make instant decisions and actions that may save lives or prevent injury is the focus of much of our scenario based training.

The Stimulated Brain and Learning

We believe that in order to train students to respond effectively in stressful situations they must be exposed to simulated law enforcement scenarios and practice appropriate responses under stress. However, there is evidence that stress-inducing stimuli may reduce learning ability.

As described previously, the brain uses two key pathways (see "High and Low Road" diagram). The high brain function of the frontal cortex receives information, analyzes it, and selects actions. This cortical pathway includes many synaptic connections that add time to the transmission process, thus slowing reaction time. The low brain route takes in the same information from the sensory thalamus and shoots it directly to the amygdala. The low brain route has fewer synaptic connections and is able to respond more quickly, but the trade-off for this quicker response is that the body tends to react to the stimulus (say, a threat) without full comprehension of its nature and severity. The amygdala is constantly monitoring our environment for signs of danger. If danger is detected, behavioral responses are initiated to deal with the fear. Thus, the fight or flight concept is invoked (LeDoux 1999).

It is not necessary for the brain to recognize a threat for a reaction to occur. Recall a time you heard a sharp, loud noise. You reacted with a defensive maneuver such as freezing, (an involuntary response) yet you still had no perception of the situation and had not identified the noise as a threat (LeDoux 1999). Thus, the body, based on this advanced sensory system of the amygdala is prepared to take action if the cortex subsequently confirms the threat, or stand down if there is no danger.

A key implication for training is that once the brain learns a coping strategy for a specific threat, the amygdala drops out of the circuit. When you know how to cope successfully, you no longer need the amygdala as fear is no longer aroused. (LeDoux 1999). Interestingly, physiological signs of amygdala stimulation such as increased heart rate also disappear.

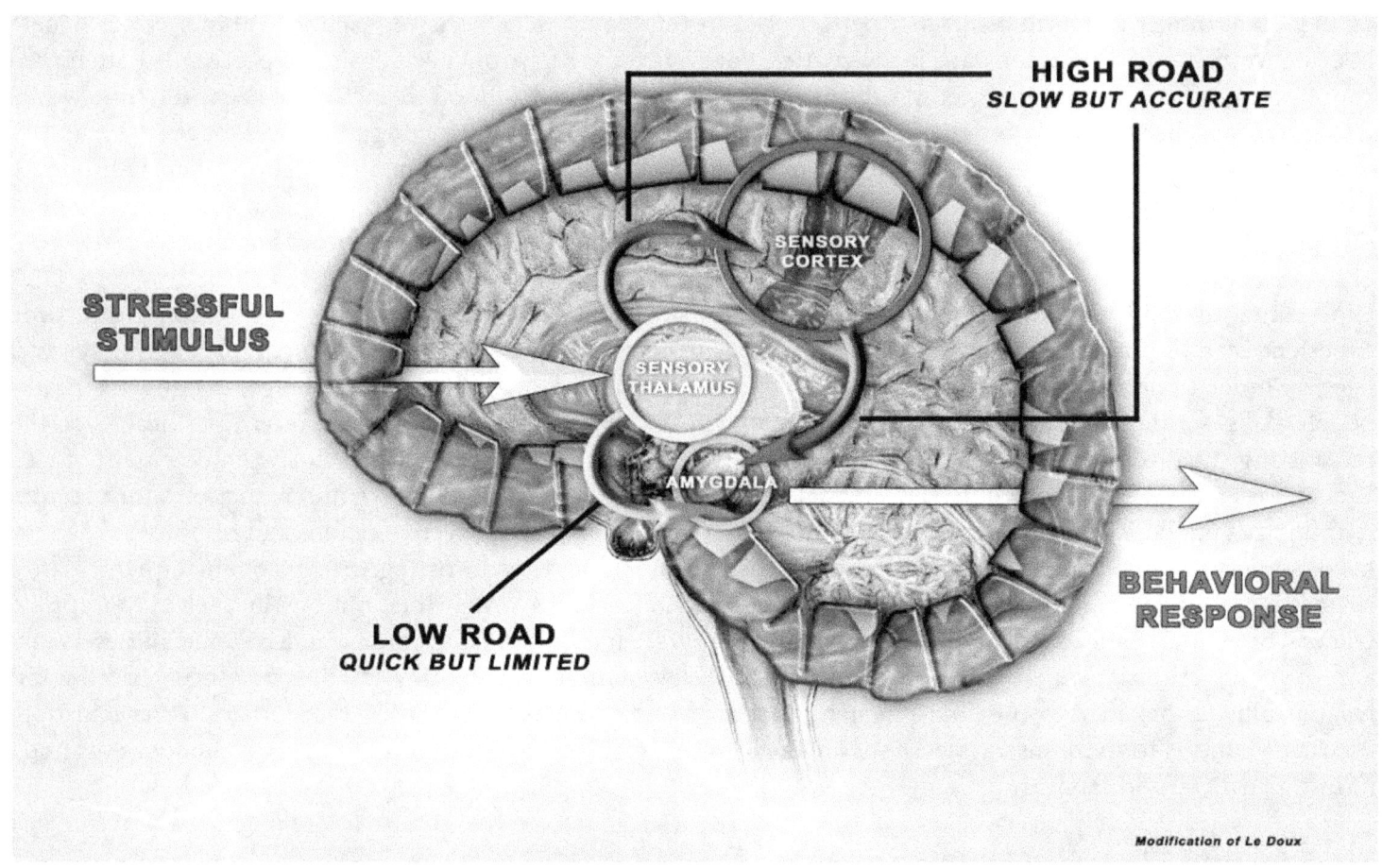

Creating Memories for Training Applications

Numerous studies by Robert Sapolsky, Bruce McEwen, Gus Pavlides, David Diamond, Tracy Shors, and Jeansok Kim indicate that stress impairs memory. This memory impairment is the result of the disruptive effects of cortisol on hippocampal activity, resulting in diminished ability to form explicit memories. Hormones released as a result of a stressful encounter have an adverse impact on the prefrontal cortex, contributing to bad decision-making under stress and these hormones also enhance the amygdala's contribution to fear (LeDoux, 1999). These hormones, then, reduce our ability to form memories, inhibit our ability to regulate fear by thinking and reasoning, and, via the amygdala, amplify our reactions to fear as well our memories of the stressful situation. Two key training implications are:

- We can store memories about potentially harmful situations

- Since we don't know what we learned from those memories due to the hormonal inhibition of thinking and reasoning, we may only learn a fear response that triggers a reaction that has not been adapted to deal appropriately with the stimulus.

Let's look at an example of this. An emotional arousal such as the sound of a large dog growling provides us with an emotional stimulus. This sound triggers the stimulus to the brain based on our memories of that stimulus. We perhaps remember the fear of a large dog, a bad encounter with a large dog. These cause an emotional arousal to the amygdala. Our previous experience with dogs does not alone trigger any specific response. The fear response is initiated only when the amygdala is stimulated. This translates into the amygdala transferring the cognition of the stimulus (the growling dog) into an emotional event. At this point, we have no working memory of how to deal with the growling dog, just the memory of the noise as something to be feared. Thus, our previously learned fear tells us to react with fear, but has not equipped us with an appropriate response to that fear. Here again, our emotions monopolize our consciousness. The brain's focus becomes dominated by the fear stimulus, and reduces our ability to process other bits of information that are coming at us (Ratey, 2002).

In the present context, our goal as trainers is to enhance our trainees' future effectiveness and safety by creating memories of appropriate reactions to stressful law enforcement scenarios that will enable trainees to draw on coping experiences that are effective.

When examining the process of memory development, there are essentially two types of memory that must be considered (LeDoux, 2002). There is working memory or short term memory and long-term or stored memory. Working memory is best depicted as that memory we use as we accumulate and assimilate information as it arrives, is sorted, categorized, and then "discarded" or "filed." An example of this would be a phone number you receive from the operator and immediately dial without benefit of writing it down. If you become distracted and focus on new activities before dialing, you will not recall the numbers. Experiments have shown we can only keep a few things in this short term memory "filing cabinet." An accepted number is seven items (LeDoux, 2002). Fortunately, the brain is able to group ideas together and create a "chunk" of information, thereby calling this "chunk" one of the seven items of information (LeDoux, 2002, Howard, 2000). Thus, the caller's name of Betty Phillips becomes not two, but one chunk of information, and the seven-digit phone number becomes one chunk of information. Consider a decision-making task. The brain has the ability to draw information out of long-term memory into working memory as we focus on the task at hand. In complex tasks this "executive" function allows us to switch from activity to activity as needed.

Learning Processes

This executive function allows us to sequence information in an organized fashion so we may integrate new information with previously learned experiences and return it to long term storage as a new memory. This process is learning, whereby an action to be carried out is actually a "memory" of already formulated plans stored in long term memory. In order to have "memories" of future actions, we must have rehearsed a variety of mental actions (Ratey, 2002). Thus, we are constantly manipulating our memories and adding new data derived from experiences to expand and refine our repertoire of potential future responses. Skills learning requires us to practice, rehearse, and integrate our physical skills and resources as necessary to formulate learned responses. With repetitive practice, we can develop our memories and our skills. Testing learners helps them remember and retrieve these memories with greater ease. Ron Fisher of Florida International University (Howard, 2000) summarized his findings of testing learners:

- Learners who take pre-tests do better on their final exams.

- Learners who take pretests using fill-in-the-blank questions perform better than those taking multiple-choice exams.

- Learners who take tests with inferential multiple choice questions do better than those who test with factual   multiple-choice questions.

Rather than formulate new learned experiences, we prefer to fit our new learning into our old experiences. As previously mentioned, our prior learning experiences impacted our reactions when the dog growled. Let's look at a non-threatening experience to better understand learning. Suppose you were to hear the following phrase, "The nurse's son greeted his mother". Typically the reader might interpret that the son is greeting his mother (the nurse) rather than the possibility the nurse is the father. This tendency is so strong in human nature that instructors should use great care when listening to students discuss their newfound knowledge, and clarify instances of inappropriate application to previous experiences and memories. However, the use of prior learning experiences is a marvelous tool to convey learning. Teaching through examples based on experiences helps students modify their memories though adaptation.

Motor Skills Learning

In motor skills learning, research performed at Johns Hopkins University determined that within the first 5-6 hours of practicing a new motor skill, the brain shifts the new instructions into long-term memory. While a subject is initially practicing and learning the new motor skill, the prefrontal cortex involved in short-term memory is active. When returning to perform the skill again 5 ½ hours later, the subject had no trouble performing the skill except this time, the cerebrum had taken over as the brain had shifted the skill into long-term memory. This would suggest that a newly learned skill could be impaired, confused, or lost if a person tries to learn a different motor skill task during this critical 5-6 hour period (Ratey, 2002). An example of this would be teaching complex motor skills such as immediate action. Primary immediate action of Tap-Rack-Re-engage represents a cognitive skill due to the proper sequencing of the action, as well as a fine motor skill of weapons manipulation. This skill is immediately followed by the instruction of secondary immediate action of Rip-Work-Tap-Rack-Re-engage. Johns Hopkins is conducting research on the mixing of skills with and without interference in the learning process. Until more is known, trainers should be cautious when teaching new skills, as mixing skills during the initial learning phase may have a negative impact on skill retention.

When we repeat a skill or answer a question correctly on an exam, we say learning has taken place. When we adapt a skill or memory to a similar situation, we say we have transferred the learning. Ideally, transfer of learning is much more effective if the 'leap' of application is not too great (Howard, 2000). For example, if you teach a student to draw his weapon when a gun is pointed at him, it is easy to make the determination to draw his weapon if a knife is pointed at him. It may be a leap for the inexperienced student to draw his weapon if someone displays a can of hairspray and a cigarette lighter. Since trainers are essentially creating new memories (or more likely, modifying old memories), we must work to create learning experiences that bridge the gaps in students' experience. We can do this by transferring learning in sequential steps through examples until students develop enough examples in memory to transfer learning on their own. Effective methods include role-play, scenario training, and small-group discussions.

Training Strategies

We've noted the impact of stress on our decision-making ability. We know we select from a very short menu of responses that we've tried before. We know that we can teach skills and responses in a training environment with practice. What we need to do now is transplant these training skills and options into memories created under stress where we can control for positive learning outcomes. The reactionary skills we ask our students to perform are exactly those; skills. Some require fine motor control, some require proper sequencing of actions, and some require life-saving movement. All require mental input. Skills training (or the mechanical aspects required to perform a task), differs from stress training. However, the degree of success in performing a given task may vary with the presence of strong stimuli. We now know how learning takes place. To optimize training effectiveness, we must integrate stressful conditions into the practice environment. Such an approach will facilitate the development of appropriate learning memories. So how effective is the training we provide? What considerations should be taken into account regarding training and performance under stress?

Training Methods

Below are several considerations put forth by Keinan and Friedland (1996) for training students to perform effectively under stress:

Information Training

What should a trainee know before participating in training? Keinan and Friedland found various studies examining the effects of students' knowledge (or lack of knowledge) about what to expect in training. Though results were mixed, there were strong indications that trainees performed better in training when fully and accurately informed as to what to expect. In this context, the knowledge extends to informing individuals what is likely to occur in stressful events and advising them of common performance errors while under stress. Recall for a moment that memories (and thus potential responses to threats) require us to modify experiences. By providing visual examples in our verbal presentations, we can help the student "wire the brain" to have on hand a perception of what might happen in the stressful situation. While they will lack the emotional experience in memory, the visual memory should enhance their ability to cope with the stimulus. Such knowledge gives trainees a perception of control. Equally important to the trainees' success is the knowledge that their stress is a normal reaction and that others have performed the tasks successfully under the stressful conditions. Such information leads to greater confidence in accomplishing challenging tasks. Keinan and Friedland suggested that information on what to expect should heighten perceived control and generate reassuring messages (emphasizing stressful reactions as normal), thus contributing to improved performance in stress training.

An example of this type of training would be the explanation of what might occur to a student encountering a role-player who suddenly charges towards them with a knife. In training, the student is told to react by drawing their weapon. In reality, the student, due to innate responses, may freeze, flee, or draw the weapon. All are natural responses in the time-frame immediately following the stimulus. Knowledge of these natural responses is essential to providing a positive learning experience.

A benefit of inclusion of this training philosophy in scenario based training is the ease with which it can be added. Creating visual images and identifying potential responses takes little time and may provide tremendous learning benefits for the student.

Intensity Training

The literature on this subject describes studies with very diverse results. Some studies of task performance under stress demonstrated improved performance under similar conditions and that training under non-stressful conditions did not improve performance under stressful conditions (Lazarus, 1966, Keinan and Friedland 1966). Conversely, other studies showed that training conducted under no especially stressful conditions produced better results than training conducted under intense stress, which resulted in decreased trainee confidence in performance. Based on their research, three elements were identified as important to successful stress training. These were 1) familiarization with potential stressors involved in the training, 2) exposure to stressors without hindering trainee confidence, and 3) stress exposure training that does not interfere with skills acquisition. They identified several training methods that meet these requirements

First is the practice of graduated training wherein the trainee starts with mild levels of stress, and is gradually exposed to more intense stress. However, research clearly indicates the trainee should not progress to a higher level of intensity unless an acceptable level of proficiency is demonstrated at the next lower level. Also emphasized is the inherent requirement to inform the trainee, in advance, of the highest level of stress that may be reached in training.

Second is the practice of phased training. Phased training first allows the trainee to learn the skills in a no-stress environment. Then the trainee is exposed to stressors without having to perform the skills. In the third phase the trainee is required to demonstrate the skills while exposed to the stressors. This method allows the trainee to become proficient in the skills, exposes the trainee to the typical stressors where performance would be expected, and finally, allows the trainee to perform the learned skills in the stressful environment. (Salas, 1996)

Overlearning

The arguments for and against overlearning are numerous. Keinan and Friedland's review of the literature found overlearning an advantage where complex tasks are concerned. Overlearning could simplify these tasks and thus make them less subject to stress. Overlearning could create automatic responses that would create less demand for attentional consideration by the performer and thus, should be less stressful. Overlearning could also instill a sense of control, thereby creating a lessened stress response for the individual. However, the potential pitfalls of overlearning are disconcerting. Research indicates overlearning may limit trainees' responses, thus inhibiting their ability to improvise. Also, overlearning tends to induce boredom and reduces motivation. Finally, overlearning may result in a number of competing dominant responses that could cause negative performance under stress.

While overlearning still may be a viable training option, Keinan and Friedland identified some safeguards that should be considered:

- Overlearning should be limited to tasks that will not change as the circumstances change. If the task varies   depending on the circumstances, overlearning can prove detrimental to the decision making process and ultimately detrimental to performance.

- Overlearning of different responses to similar stimuli should be avoided as performance proves difficult under stress.

- Fatigue and boredom often accompany overlearning. Training should be challenging. Competitiveness can assist the trainer in creating the challenge.

Skill training

Skill training is used to lessen the effects of stress by producing overlearned behavior. "Well-rehearsed tasks are less prone to degradation under conditions of stress; well rehearsed tasks become 'automatic', thus requiring less of the individual's attention; and well drilled tasks enhance a person's sense of predictability and control" (Driskell and Salas, 1991; Logan, 1985; Salas). This was found to be true for procedural tasks such as disassembly of an M60 machine gun in a study conducted by Schendel and Hagman. The results showed an overtrained group made 65% fewer errors than a control group when retested after 8 weeks. While physical skills are readily responsive to repetitive testing, cognitive skills apparently are more perishable. Consider the findings of Driskell, Willis and Copper that found, "the longer the delay between the overlearning and performance, the weaker the overlearning effect, with the benefits in performance reduced by one-half after 19 days" (Orasanu and Backer, 1996).

Another benefit of skill training is that it helps to generate students' perception of the benefits of the training. Two studies cited by Orasanu and Backer indicate that the type of training may motivate individuals to perform under stressful conditions. In one study a group soldiers were aware their training would involve lethal agents. The other group was trained in a non-lethal environment. On written exams both groups achieved similar scores. The first group however, had the perception that they were better prepared to perform if under chemical attack. A second study concluded "exposure to serious physical threats during training yielded better training results than training that did not involve such threats only when the soldiers concluded their training with a feeling of success." From this study, it appears that individual perceptions and differences are strongly related to performance under stress (Orasanu and Backer, 1996).

Stress Exposure Training (SET)

The Naval Air Warfare Center (NAWC) and Dr. Joan Hall (1996) have been pro-active in developing training models that train for high stress tasks. Stress Exposure Training (SET) was designed to answer the need to teach cognitive/behavioral stress coping skills to service personnel. This training embodies three basic components. These are 1) coping skills to re-channel negative thoughts into positive thoughts and reactions, 2) problem-solving skills, and 3) the use of deep breathing to counter physiological effects of stress. These skills are then practiced in simulated stressful environments. The NAWC cited 17 studies showing SET training had a positive effect on cognitive or psychomotor performance (Development of Instructional Design Guidelines for Stress Exposure Training. J. K. Hall et al., NAWC).

Important to the development of SET training is the clear identification of the types of stressors encountered and the performance objectives. Hall, et. al. outlined the need for a stress analysis, akin to a task analysis, to identify typical stressors encountered, performance deficiencies likely to occur, knowledge, skills, and abilities required to perform the duties, and any cues in the environment that trigger use of stress coping skills.

Stress Inoculation Training

Stress Inoculation Training includes the following educational, rehearsal, and application stages (Orasanu and Backer, 1996):

- Education phase - "People learn about the different ways in which people respond to different types of stress."

- Rehearsal stage - "individuals learn one on a number of stress management techniques most applicable to their particular situation." These include relaxation, deep breathing, guided imagery, and stretching.

- Application stage - "individuals apply techniques they have learned. First in a simulated environment, then an actual stressful environment."

Scenario Training

Many basic skills can be learned in classroom situations and in field practice. The majority of successful models examined here require individuals to train and

be tested under realistic, stressful conditions in order to assure effective performance under stressful conditions. Feedback should be provided promptly to students during this realistic training, directing them toward the desired responses. This feedback is held in short term (electrical and neurotransmitter-mediated) memory circuits, and may or may not be consolidated into long term memory to be available for future challenges. Consolidation and retention involves lasting synaptic modification, which requires protein synthesis. The occurrence of consolidation can only be confirmed by testing for specific recall of the training material. Appropriate re-testing can reinforce the learning, as it strengthens synaptic connectivity (de Kloet, 1999).

RESEARCH DESIGN

Performance and Physiological/Psychological Factors

A review of the literature helped set the precept for the research design. As noted, physiological responses to stress include increases in heart rate, blood pressure, and cortisol. Existing research suggests the potential responses for an individual involved in a stressful encounter. Siddle (1998) identified certain factors that may impede an individual's capacity for optimal performance in stressful situations. The research indicated that heart rate plays a major factor in one's ability to react. During stress, the heart rate increases and the body shifts its resources to survival functions. As attention shifts from threat perception to threat response, one may fail to process information needed to make appropriate decisions. One's focus may become seriously narrowed, and fine motor skills may rapidly deteriorate. Our instinctive behavior for survival may overtake us, and we may therefore react in sub-optimal ways to the situation. Easterbrook's Cue-Utilization Hypothesis suggests that the individual is assumed to take in cues from the environment or from his own movements that aid in future performances. As arousal increases there is a reduction of cues used to regulate performance. At some optimal level of arousal, the most effective combination of attention to relevant cues seems to exist. However, when the arousal level is further increased, there is a further restriction in the range of cues used, many relevant cues are not included, and performance deteriorates.

This research further reported that performance is optimized when the heart rate is between 115 and 145 beats per minute. Here, an individual can perform with ease a variety of fine motor skills such as loading a weapon. As the heart rate increases, the individual experiences a deterioration of fine motor skills as well as their complex motor skills. Complex motor skills include chambering a round, handcuffing a suspect, and performing weapons retention maneuvers.

The HeartMath Research Center subjected police officers to typical threat-based scenarios and measured the heart rates and evaluated the performances of officers immediately following scenario training. The heart rate recordings show that it takes the body a considerable amount of time to recover from such intense levels of stress. In this group of officers, results showed that on average, heart rate remained elevated well above baseline for more than one hour after the scenario debriefing (HeartMath Research Center, 1999).

Siddle uses a unique law enforcement interpretation of the term "hypervigilance." In his book *Sharpening the Warrior's Edge* (Siddle, 1998) he describes hypervigilance as "catastrophic failure of the cognitive processing capabilities, leading to fatal increase of reaction time (freezing in place, failure to remember training, failure to perceive important factors or irrational acts)." Thus, the term "hypervigilance" is used to denote what others might call "panic" or "hyperarousal." In this state, individuals are said to make seriously flawed judgments. These terms may also explain the statistic that only 21% of all rounds fired by police officers hit the intended target in an encounter (FBI Uniform Crime Report, 2000).

It is necessary to note the stress reaction **can** be induced in a simulated environment. Speilberger et al., (1993) defined the stress reaction as **the emotional reaction or response that is evoked when a person perceives a particular situation as personally dangerous or frightening to him, irrespective of the presence or absence of a real objective danger.**

Research Goal

Using this information as a framework for the research, the study sought to assess a law enforcement trainee's ability to perform appropriately under the influence of high-risk (potential for lethal threat) encounters. Accordingly, we developed a human performance paradigm to:

- permit measurement of physiological and psychological indicators of arousal and their impact on performance in a training environment simulating real-life, high-risk, highly stressful situations; and

- identify elements for development of a "survival score index" that could be used to assess a law enforcement trainee's ability to survive a threat encounter. This score will be used to address individual training deficiencies and identify areas in which the officer/agent might concentrate their future continuing professional education.

To that end we selected tasks clearly identified as objectives in the officer/agent training program which the student had already completed. We integrated 97 of these tasks into a fast-flowing, realistic scenario in such a way as to allow the measurement of several cognitive, physiological (stress indices) and psychological responses, as well as performance scores, at frequent time intervals. In this scenario we measured trainees' responses to stress, elements of performance such as perception, threat recognition, judgment, latency to respond, performance skill scores, and finally, resilience of performance under stressful conditions. The paradigm was made stressful by:

- adding environmental distracters (e.g. noise, time pressure, peer pressure and "lethal" threat in actual combat with simunitions).

- providing the subject with a fixed number of cues that facilitate recognition and the escalation of the threat.

- undermining the assumed social supports (subject's "partner" is a confederate of the experimenters, and will make critical errors in the scenario; backup, if requested will not be available).

- multitask loading (student must radio for backup while simultaneously seeking cover in the midst of a firefight).

- minimizing resources (e.g. minimal cover in shooting situation, weapon rigged to misfire). [It should be noted that the student had previously received training specifically covering: high-speed driving, combat against role players using simunitions, finding and using available cover as well as specific drills on how to correct a weapons malfunction.]

Scenario Design

The scenario incorporated realism drawn from actual experiences of law enforcement subject matter experts. Role players (instructional staff) were used for interaction with the trainee during the scenario. The trainee's partner was introduced as an "advanced training student" also participating in the scenario for the first time. This partner was, in fact, an instructor whose role was clearly defined to help control the movements of the basic trainee. The student responded to a series of dispatched activities which served to control the time and sequence of the scenario. The actions of the trainee and partner were monitored and video recorded to more precisely evaluate stress reactions and shifts in both psychological and physiological responses. The scenario was broken into 7 "events" denoted by clear transitions in the nature of the activity and the level of arousal indicated by the event. Brief descriptions of these events follow:

1. Call in service – lowest level of stress used to establish radio communications abilities.

2. Non-Emergency Vehicle Operation driving re-test – provided escalating stress as the effect of testing is introduced.

3. Emergency Vehicle Operation – escalating stress as the trainee is asked to complete the high-speed qualification course within the same testing parameters of the actual training test given three weeks previously. A driver training instructor graded the trainee's performance.

4. Spin-out – potentially high stress level as the clearly inept "senior partner" (a driver training instructor) appears to lose control of the vehicle and spins "out of control" and off the course at high speed.

5. Entry to the building – provides some de-escalation in the levels of arousal as the officer/agents leave the driving range to back up a supervisory officer in trouble and enter a building to take what is identified as a routine report. The scenario required the trainee to take a routine report of theft from a cooperative complainant as the supervisor leaves the scene.

6. Gun take-away/shootout – maximum levels of arousal were achieved as the scenario deteriorates with the return of the theft suspect, an escalating argument, and the decision by the "senior partner" to remove the hostile theft suspect from the building. The "senior partner" has his weapon taken and is shot by the suspect, who then takes the complainant hostage which he also shoots. Stress is further escalated by loud music limiting communication, the sound of a loud, barking dog in the adjoining room, very close quarters and very limited cover. The exit is blocked by the downed "body" of the "senior partner." The suspect (a firearms instructor) has cover and produces a shotgun (simunitions) which he uses in conjunction with the downed "senior partner's" weapon to fire at exposed parts of the trainee with simunitions rounds. The trainee's third round in the magazine in the weapon provided has been altered to not fire, forcing the trainee to respond to the development. The suspect is either shot by the officer and eventually falls, or commits suicide if the officer does not disable the suspect.

7. Response to an internal affairs interview – de-escalating stress. Once out-of-role is called and weapons surrendered, an immediate "post-shooting" interview is conducted with questions including justification for actions, recall of the events, and recall of training.

In these seven events performance attributes included: emergency vehicle operation, perception of surroundings (presence of innocent civilians, availability of cover), threat assessment, verbal communications (clear and appropriate to circumstances and individuals), and firearms skills (safety, weapon retention, management of weapon malfunction, accuracy), as well as post-event ability to recall and describe actions. Scenario testing took an average of 35 minutes per student. All scenario activity was recorded on video tape via a multitude of fixed cameras.

Participants had completed all pertinent portions of the FLETC training program, which included, in addition to intensive didactic instruction, numerous practical training exercises on specific tasks, including: field interviewing techniques, radio communications, emergency and non-emergency driving, firearms safety and target shooting, interactive target shooting (including shoot/no-shoot judgment situations), managing subject non-compliance (passive resistance, unarmed assault, knife attacks attempts to take officers' weapon and assault on officers with firearms). Interactive practical exercises involving instructors as role players included use of non-lethal techniques (hand-to-hand, baton and pepper spray) as well as lethal force practice involving exchange of fire with armed role players at close range using simunitions.

Subjects

The participants for this study were selected from the total volunteer population of 1268 law enforcement students attending basic law enforcement training at the Federal Law Enforcement Training Center located at Glynco, Georgia. Participants were selected from two distinct career paths: criminal investigators or uniformed officers. Criminal investigators are provided basic and fundamental training in the techniques, concepts, and methodologies of conducting criminal investigations. Uniformed officers are provided a study of basic law enforcement concepts that a new officer should understand and/or be able to perform upon employment in a Federal law enforcement organization.

Participants ranged from 21 to 51 years, with a mean of 29.37. There were 100 participants (83% male and 17% female) and no subjects were excluded due to age or sex. The participants' education ranged from 17% with High School diplomas, 7% with Associate degrees, 54% with Baccalaureate degrees, and 20% with Graduate degrees. They represented diverse ethnic backgrounds (67% were White, 13% were Black, 10% were Hispanic, 7% were Asian/Pacific Islander, and 2% were American Indian/Alaskan). Subjects were excluded from the study if they had consumed caffeine products or smoked within 2 hours prior to any of the physiological assessments. Also, volunteers were excluded if they had a medical problem or were taking any of the medications on the prohibited medication list.

All participants were informed about the procedures and gave written consent before participating in the study. There were no specific diagnostic criteria required for entry, and all participants were required to complete a personal history questionnaire as well as completing the State Trait assessment prior to enrollment. Only volunteers were selected for inclusion in the study.

Instruments

Physiological values (heart rate, blood pressure, and saliva) were measured before, during, and after the scenario. An Accutracker II ™ (SunTech Medical Corp) was used to measure blood pressure and heart rate during the scenario. A Polar Accurex Plus™ heart rate monitor and wrist watch continuously stored heart rate levels throughout the testing. The watch face was taped over to eliminate feedback to the wearer. All values were downloaded and analyzed at the conclusion of testing.

Salivary cortisol was collected by means of a salivette cotton swab, which was saturated in the mouth for two minutes, stored in collection tubes, and frozen for subsequent analysis. Four specimens were taken: (1) at the start of baseline orientation, (2) at the start of the scenario, (3) immediately after the scenario, and (4) 30 minutes after completion of the scenario. Saliva samples were assayed for cortisol by the Walter Reed Army Institute of Research (WRAIR).

Psychological responses were estimated via self-report questionnaires administered before and after the scenario. The instruments used to measure personality traits were the State Trait Personality Inventory (STPI) State Trait Anger Expression Inventory (STAXI-2) (Orientation, Baseline, Pre-Scenario, and Scenario), and the Lie (L)-Scale of the Minnesota Multiphasic Personality Inventory-2 (MMPI-2). The State-Trait Personality Inventory (STPI) is a self-report inventory measuring state and trait anxiety, anger, depression, and curiosity. The state and trait scales differ in item wording and response format, to report the intensity of these emotional states and frequency of the corresponding personality traits. The STPI S-Anxiety scale was constructed to measure the intensity of anxiety as an emotional state, with low scores indicating feeling calm and serene, intermediate scores indicating moderate levels of tension and worry, and high scores reflecting intense anxiety, approaching terror and panic. The STPI Trait-Anxiety (T-Anxiety) scale assesses individual differences in the tendency to perceive a wide range of situations as dangerous or threatening, especially situations that involve evaluation by other individuals or threats to self-esteem. Individuals high in T-Anxiety respond to perceived threats with more frequent and intense elevations in State-Anxiety (S-Anxiety) than individuals low in T-Anxiety. Stronger anxiety trait scores indicate the probability that the individual will experience intense elevations of state anxiety when faced with a threatening situation. The STPI anger scales assess the intensity and frequency that anger is expressed. *State anger (S-Anger) is defined as a psychobiological state or condition consisting of subjective feelings that vary in intensity, from mild irritation or annoyance to intense fury and rage, with concomitant activation or arousal of the autonomic nervous system* (Spielberger, 1999). S-Anger fluctuates over time as a function of perceived affronts, injustice, or frustration. Trait anger (T-Anger) is defined in terms of individual differences in the frequency that S-Anger is experienced over time; individuals high in T-Anger perceive a wider range of situations as anger provoking (e.g., annoying, irritating, frustrating) than those low in T-Anger and more frequently experience elevations in S-Anger whenever such conditions are encountered. The STPI curiosity scales assess curiosity as an emotional state and individual differences as a personality trait. State curiosity is closely linked to State anxiety in that individuals high in state curiosity and low in state anxiety are exploration motivated (i.e. thrill seekers). However, when state anxiety is higher than state curiosity, individuals tend to display avoidance behavior (i.e., flight reactions). Individuals with high trait curiosity experience curiosity states with more frequency and at higher intensities than those with lower trait curiosity scores. High state and trait scores typically manifest themselves among individuals who tend to seek information and experience or sensation. While not a primary focus of this research, the STPI depression scales assess depression as an emotional state and individual differences as a personality trait. Depression is associated with both anxiety and anger in that depressed individuals typically experience high levels of anxiety and intense anger. These feelings are often reflected as low self-esteem and hopelessness.

Administration of STPI and STAXI Inventories

The combined STPI and STAXI were administered in three phases: (1) to 1268 basic training students at the start of their program; (2) to the 182 students who volunteered for the study during the seventh or eighth week of their training program; (3) to 100 randomly selected volunteers upon their arrival to participate in the research scenario (Pre-Scenario). The STPI state scales were also administered to the 100 subjects at the conclusion of the interview portion of the scenario (Post-Scenario). The MMPI-2 was used to detect a deliberate attempt to present oneself in a favorable light.

Evaluation

Videotapes were used to assess performance by a team of subject matter experts. Participants' responses were measured on elements of performance such as perception, threat recognition, judgment, latency to respond, performance skill scores, and finally, resilience of performance under stressful conditions. In all, the research team collected data on 368 variables. The following forms were created to collect and record the data:

Demographic Data Information Questionnaire collected variables such as age, sex, education, race, and previous law enforcement and military experience.

Shot Placement Report recorded the number of hits to the suspect as well as whether the participant had cleared the weapon properly.

Heart Rate/Blood Pressure Recording Sheet recorded the activity/event, time (in minutes/seconds), blood pressure (systolic & diastolic values), and heart rate.

Scenario Performance Event Evaluation Sheet. The scenario was divided into seven events and included 97 measurable tasks extracted from training lesson plans. Participants were evaluated on multiple performance requirements in each event. Lesson plans and their enabling performance objectives were identified and reviewed during the development of the scenario. The scenario's seven major sub-parts included:

1. "Call In-Service" (4 tasks)
2. "Complete a Non-Emergency Vehicle Operations (NEVO) course" (3 tasks)
3. "Complete an Emergency Vehicle Response Course" (27 tasks)
4. "Spin-Out" (7 tasks)
5. "Enter Building" (14 tasks)
6. "Gun Take Away/Shootout" (24 tasks)
7. "Response to an Internal Affairs Interview" (14 tasks).

The performance requirements for each task were "Go/No-Go or N/A (not applicable)." In addition to the performance requirements there were two response time scores measured: (1) Response time to the dispatchers call after the spin-out and (2) Response time after the suspect takes the partner's weapons. The scenario was designed to be "winnable," with the suspect committing suicide if the officer failed to or was unable to continue to engage the suspect.

Equipment

Participants were provided with a remote transmitter microphone (clipped to their lapel), a police radio, handcuffs, 3 magazines (with 10 rounds each of simunitions), magazine pouches and holster, and a Sig Sauer 9mm semiautomatic pistol modified to fire simunitions. Standard training safety equipment included a vest with groin protection, helmet with simunitions face shield with throat protector, and Kevlar shooting gloves. Prior to the start of the scenario, a video was shown to the trainees informing them of safety guidelines.

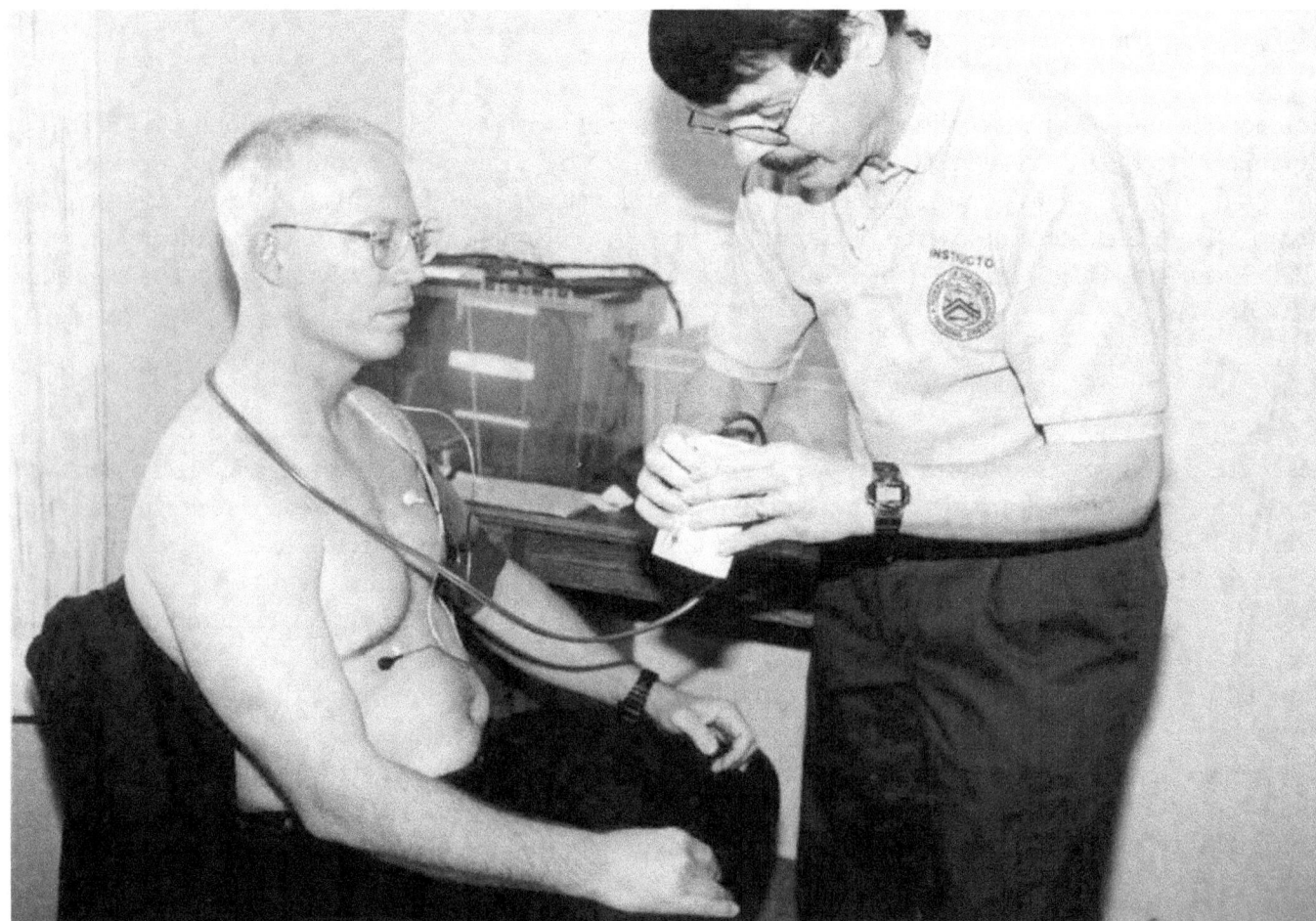

RESEARCH FINDINGS

THE RESEARCH SCENARIO

The research scenario was developed to evaluate performance and decision making skills of FLETC trainees in a high stress environment. The goal of this study was to address the following research questions:

- Can we validate our training scenarios as being realistic/highly stressful? Trainees are asked to perform law enforcement skills in scenarios that replicate real world situations that are stressful. This component will compare the stress response of trainees in this study to the stress response measured in other studies designed to elicit an acute stress response.

- Can specific psychological factors be identified that predict performance in a highly stressful law enforcement encounter?

- Can specific physiological factors be identified that predict performance in a highly stressful law enforcement encounter?

- Can specific physiological factors be used to identify an "optimum stress level for optimum performance" as suggested by various authors?

- What effect does high stress have on decision-making (cognitive processing)?

Once specific factors have been identified and the results of this study discussed with the many trainers and subject matter experts, we will then focus on the second phase of this research endeavor which will focus on answering the more far-reaching question:

How can these identified factors be used to improve/modify instruction at FLETC, and thereby, improve performance under stress?

TRAINING FINDINGS

SUMMARY OF THE 7 EVENTS

EVENT 1 – Call In-Service

Event one provided the source of performance and physiological data based on routine activities for the research study. The low-demand requirements for proper radio communications procedures, calling in-service in a timely fashion and responding appropriately to the dispatcher were met with a high degree of success. Overall, event one reflected a 93% pass rate for all trainees tested. Radio communications showed 97.9% of the trainees passing.

LINEAR TREND OF PERCENT CHANGE IN ALL VALUES - GRAPH 1

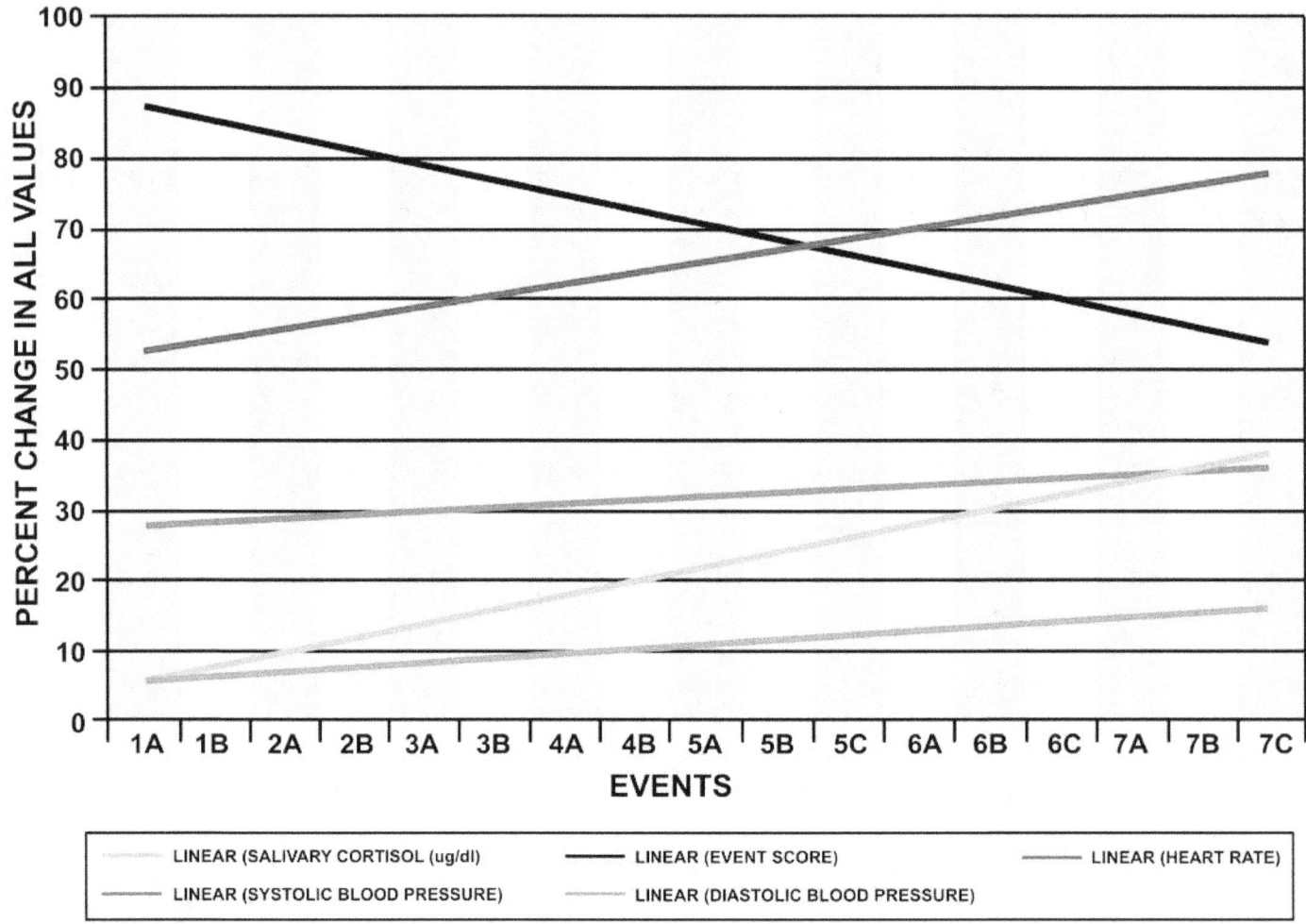

Graph 1 identifies each of the events in the research scenario. Heart rate, systolic and diastolic blood pressure baseline values were compared to those collected at the beginning (1A) and end (7C) of the scenario. Cortisol values compare the pre-scenario value (just before 1A) to event 7C. Event scores reflect the trend of performance levels as the scenario proceeded. There is a possible score of 100% for each the 97 measured elements and based on "go/no-go" scoring. The overall performance score was achieved by examining the "go/no-go" scores for each of the 97 elements, applying the Federal Law Enforcement Training Center standard of 70% as a passing score, and reducing the 97 elements to one number.

EVENT 2 – Non-Emergency Vehicle Operation (NEVO)

Event 2 examined radio communication procedures and Non-Emergency Vehicle Operation (NEVO). This event was staged to increase the stress level. First, the trainees were told they were going to be tested. Second, they were instructed to drive on a non-emergency vehicle operation course they had never seen before. Third, the time given to complete the course in order to achieve a passing score was purposely insufficient so as to increase stress. The overall event score showed only a 79.55% pass rate. A closer examination of the individually scored elements indicates the trainees had a fairly high success rate on the NEVO course for techniques (i.e. did not hit the cones), but the trainees failed the course due to the insufficient time limits. Overall, the trainees were successful in performing the skills portion of the NEVO with an average score of 89% during the scenario.

Radio communications was evaluated in this exercise, and trainees showed a high level of success in passing evaluated elements of radio communications with 93.9% of the trainees passing.

EVENT 3 – Emergency Response (Trainee as Driver)

Event three examined the trainees on the emergency response (ER) course. This event was anticipated to increase stress levels beyond that of the NEVO course. Unlike the NEVO course, the trainees were tested on the same range they had previously qualified on for a comparison of retention of skills. The event was scored as it was scored in the training environment.

First, each trainee was scored on the basis of skill, which includes techniques and the proper line of travel through the turns. During the scenario, trainees achieved an average score of 86.58% for line of travel and technique compared to the training average score of 91.28%. This five point reduction in score occurred three weeks after their driver training test, and may be of interest for further research concerning the time period of skill retention.

Second, the trainees showed a decrease in ability to pass within the qualifying time limits. Trainees were tested on the appropriate course for their program and that each had successfully qualified (passed) on three weeks prior. In this phase of the scenario, only 67% passed in the allotted time. These scores suggest the trainees are able to retain their skills (achieving a passing score only five points lower than the qualifying score), but the speed with which they were able to execute those skills diminished at a faster rate.

Of interest is the comparison between training groups, which actually represent the two training programs / curricula. One group must drive the course approximately 10 seconds faster than the other group to achieve a passing score. All trainees took an average of 7 seconds longer to complete the course when compared to their actual driving times in basic training This data suggests trainees in both groups diminish at the same rate from the set standard. Strong inference exists as to the desirability of having trainees train to the higher standard in some activities, as the rate of diminishing ability is comparable between the two groups.

Radio communications scores remain relatively high with 94.8% of the trainees passing.

EVENT 4 – Spin-out (Trainee as passenger)

This event was designed to continue the escalation of stress for the trainees. The event found the trainee in the passenger seat for emergency response, and relegated to handling all radio communications. All radio communications and communications with the partner occur IMMEDIATELY AFTER the vehicle spins out at high speed (when the car comes to a rest after the spin-out the dispatcher calls the unit). Overall trainee performance shows only 28.28% of the trainees succeeded (met the response requirement) in this event. Only 68.7% of the trainees passed the radio communications performance measures. This rapid decrease in communication skills was recorded as was the concurrent elevation of heart rate and systolic blood pressure. Once the dispatcher calls immediately after the spin-out, the trainee is required to answer the radio within 8 seconds to receive a "go" for this measure. After 20 seconds and two calls from the dispatcher go unanswered, the senior partner is instructed to tell the trainee to answer the radio. This prompting response provided consistency to the scenario, but undoubtedly altered the true response time that would have been observed had the prompting not occurred. The trainees averaged 9.5 seconds to recognize and respond to their call sign after the spin-out. These scores provide additional confirmation that communication skills and cognitive processes diminish under events of high stress.

EVENT 5 – Arrive at scene/Enter house to take report

This event is used as a transition between event 4 and 6. It was necessary to allow a de-escalation of stress in order to get the trainees to enter the scenario building (in accordance with principles of training). This was accomplished by having the trainee and partner respond to an officer needing assistance. Upon arrival, they discover that the supervisor on scene had a radio malfunction and needed a routine report to be taken. Once inside and while taking a report from a cooperative person, the stress level for the trainee was again increased with loud music, the sound of a barking dog, and an escalating argument when the suspect returns to the scene. The trainees were evaluated in communications, officer presence, and trainee response in controlling the situation as it evolved.

Overall, the trainees posted an average score of 39.39% for this event. The trainees performed well in the areas of officer presence and in escalation of force by responding appropriately, creating distance and taking controlling measures. The skills observed demonstrated the trainees were well prepared to handle escalating confrontations, understood the principles of teamwork in a law enforcement environment, and were conscious of their actions and responses to the growing threat. They were fully engaged in the role and used verbal commands and physical skills to control the actions of the complainant. Their low scores in this event can be attributed to communications skills that lowered the overall score considerably. Radio procedures and communication with the dispatcher were very poor with only 42% passing these elements. They simply did not use the radio to call for assistance, and when they were called by the dispatcher they failed to respond or responded incorrectly. Some even handed the radio to their partner to respond even though the partner was dealing with the more volatile suspect while the trainee had the cooperative complainant. The general response pattern indicated that in order to focus actions and responses on the escalating hostilities, the trainees no longer considered other alternatives such as the use of the radio with its potential benefits of summoning assistance. They seem to have focused on events in their presence and prioritized these events as requiring their undivided attention. This decrease in decision making ability (perceptual narrowing) is a classic manifestation of the stress response.

EVENT 6 – Gun take-away and shoot-out

Event 6 was designed to invoke maximum stress levels. Overall, performance, deteriorated, as expected, and only 28.2% performed well enough to pass this event.. Several stress producing elements were placed in this event. The "startle" response was invoked here, as the gun take-away and shooting occur rapidly and in a confined area with little cover and no avenue of retreat. As a result, this phase of the overall scenario saw the highest blood pressure and heart rates recorded during the seven events.

Popular theory has long held that a loss of fine and complex motor skill could be observed as a result of high stress levels. The trainees observed in this study did not appear to be unable to perform fine and complex motor skills as noted when weapons handling skills were evaluated. Rather, they seemed to perform them in the incorrect sequence or perform the wrong function all together, thereby producing a 25.8% success rate. Many of the trainees tapped the top or side of the weapon as the first stage of the immediate action drill, rather than the bottom of the magazine. A number merely racked the slide. More than a few would shoot, work the slide, and shoot until the weapon was empty, sometimes pulling the trigger up to 10 times before initiating a reload. Loading exercises were performed smoothly, though every single trainee turned their total attention to the weapon and the reload rather than maintaining contact with the suspect as per their training. This inability to perform skills was observed to be more the result of impaired decision-making (mental) ability rather than impaired motor capability. The low performance scores reflected this impaired decision making capacity.

Further evidence of poor decision-making was noted in the trainee maintaining the position of advantage (51% passing). The speed of the engagement and proximity of the threat forced the trainees into situations requiring rapid decision-making. While virtually all trainees sought cover, the cover that was provided was minimal. Rather than maintain minimal cover, many trainees left cover and exposed themselves further by turning their backs to the suspect, charging the suspect while the suspect was shooting at them, or stepping into the middle of the room to engage the suspect from a more direct angle. Summary scores for EVENT 6 include:

Successful performance (70% and above) was recorded in the areas of:

- Threat assessment (73.2%)
- 100% correct in judgment to shoot (70.2%)
- Consistent with use of force continuum (79.2%)
- Performed emergency reload at least once correctly (72.0%)
- Continues to engage the suspect (76.8%)
- Responded to call sign accurately –Post shooting (73.5%)
- Operated radio correctly- post shooting (70.4%)
- Responded to call sign timely- post shooting (71.2%)

These results indicate most of the trainees did recognize the man with the gun who had a hostage and shot the partner as a threat, used appropriate force (firearms) against that threat, and continued to engage the suspect. With two opportunities to reload, the trainees generally recognized when the slide was locked to the rear, dropped the magazine and inserted a loaded magazine. The three remaining elements were post-shooting communications activities that occurred after the threat was neutralized.

Mid-range performance (50%-70%) was recorded in the areas of:

- Maintains position of advantage (51.0%)
- Maintains officer presence (68.1%)
- Properly identify when to shoot (57.9%)
- Verbal commands utilized (68.4%)
- Exercised tactical retreat (50.5%)
- During scenario gave follow-up identifier –post shooting (55.6%)
- During scenario gave follow-up details- post shooting (52.2%)
- Called EMS for downed partner –post shooting (63.1%)
- Handled radio in weak hand –post shooting (65.7%)

These data show a majority of the trainees presented themselves as in a position of authority, could identify when to shoot, gave verbal commands, and considered or appeared to consider a tactical retreat. The four post-shooting elements were all communications related.

Low performance (under 50%) was recorded in the areas of:

- Used proper tactics to control the suspect (30.1%)
- Performed immediate action (30.2%)
- Performed tactical reload (7.1%)
- Performed tactical magazine exchange-3 trainees tried (0.0%)
- Demonstrated proper weapons handling (25.8%)
- Incorporated tactical movement (14.0%)
- Used proper kneeling position (9.2%)

These scores show a majority of the trainees made poor tactical decisions as to courses of action, did not effectively resort to more advanced/complex and less utilized re-loading methods, could not perform a sequence skill under stress, did not employ tactical movement concepts of "shoot and move", and did not use the instructed kneeling position behind cover.

Radio communication scores were tracked throughout the scenario and the event 6 score for radio communication shows a rise in success to 64.9% from the previous event. It should be noted the radio skills measures were expected to take place AFTER the shooting had come to and end and the suspect was down. The trainee was then expected to call for EMS and support, responding to the dispatcher's questions as appropriate. These trainees, though still observably stressed by the events, were no longer dealing with a direct threat, but were still exhibiting the physiological effects of the stress response.

EVENT 7 – Interview/debrief

Event 7 was the debrief exercise, conducted immediately post-shooting in order to determine the effects of stress on cognitive responses. The overall score shows a passing rate of 49.49%. While the trainees were observed to accurately recall and relate information that occurred prior to the event 6 (gun take-away), their ability to accurately relay information after the take-away was more noticeably inaccurate. Trainees repeatedly indicated (wrongly) the steps they had performed to clear the malfunction when, in fact those steps did not occur. Several trainees rendered visual hand movements sequencing tap-rack-reengage, recalling their training in a convincing manner while the videotapes showed those actions had clearly not occurred.

Although trainees demonstrated proper use of force 70% of the time in the scenario, it could only be articulated 57% of the time during the de-brief. Evaluators viewed the tapes to determine if the student demonstrated 100% correct judgment to shoot. The 30% that failed did so for such actions as shooting the hostage, shooting when the target disappeared behind the wall, failing to shoot though they had the opportunity when their partner was shot, or repeatedly shooting the suspect after he was down and inactive.

Further evidence indicating a lack of judgment was noted by the relatively slow response time in drawing the weapon. A time value was collected once the gun was taken away from the senior officer in the full view of the trainee. The trainees took an average of four seconds to draw their weapons and bring it up in the direction of the threat. No part of their training allows four seconds to draw and cover a threat. It was clear when the tapes were reviewed that the trainees lacked recognition and/or comprehension of the events in front of them during those first few seconds. Although they saw a gun (their partner's) suddenly appear, it apparently took several seconds for the significance of this action to register in their mind.

The use of force was successfully articulated by 57% of the trainees, as they correctly described the moment they perceived lethal force could be properly used. The remaining 43% typically could only identify that they had the ability to shoot when the suspect pointed the gun at them. These trainees, though prompted to consider this further, could not articulate the gun take-away, the shot partner, or the hostage at gun-point as actions worthy of the use of lethal force.

The results for Event 7 verify the numerous limiting effects stress exerts on cognitive perception, recall, and decision making skills.

SHOT PLACEMENT

Shot placement data was collected immediately following event 6. The specific performance elements recorded were weapons clearing, number of rounds saved, shots placed on the suspect, and shot placement on the suspect Overall performance in this element showed a 28% passing rate. Analysis determined only 3.4% of the trainees demonstrated 70% accuracy or better when all rounds expended during the engagement were considered. Only 19.4% of all rounds fired hit the suspect who was approximately 3 yards from the trainee. In addition to shots going low, trainees scored poorly in applying fire to center mass or available center mass. Approximately 20% shot the hostage. The only performance item in the upper 50 percentile was proper clearing on the weapon, with 63% passing this element.

Of note was the statistically significant difference in overall shot placement scores by gender. 94.74% of females failed the shot placement element, while 66.25% of males failed. Further analysis was conducted to examine firearms qualification scores achieved during training. Once again, a statistically significant difference was, observed (as expected), with females averaging 248 compared to 273 for males. These data would suggest that a lower degree of accuracy in a static training environment may translate into a lower level of accuracy in a dynamic environment.

DEMOGRAPHICS

Demographics data were collected on each trainee and reflected gender, age, marital status, parental status, hobbies, law enforcement experience, and military experience. These data were compared to program of instruction, performance, heart rate, blood pressure, and cortisol levels. The findings were largely insignificant, showing the group to be fairly homogenous. Differences in gender and shot placement were statistically significant and have previously been addressed. Law enforcement and military experience was shown to be a factor during the driving skills portion of the scenario and the evaluation of shot placement. Differences in law enforcement experience in event 3 (NEVO) showed those with law enforcement experience did better than those without. The difference was statistically significant at the .04 level. Further analysis indicated physiological data had no impact on these differences. It is assumed those with law enforcement experience may have experience in driving police sedans. The law enforcement advantage was again found to be significant in event 4 (Emergency response) at the .02 level. Finally, law enforcement experience proved an advantage for the overall score of shot placement. Those with prior law enforcement recorded a 37.31% pass rate compared to non-law enforcement personnel who posted a 9.68% pass rate. The difference was statistically significant at the .004 level.

COGNITIVE SCORE

A cognitive score was extracted from the 97 elements by grouping 24 elements that required decision-making of the trainee during the scenario. Examples of elements include: threat assessment, identify when to shoot, used verbal commands, and maintains position of advantage. These did not include such items as driving skills, operation of the radio, reloads, or weapons clearing. Of the 100 trainees examined, 65.7% failed. Some of the elements were rated on trainee performance during the entire event. An example would be if, in event 6, the trainee used good cover most of the time but at one point turned their back on the suspect to try to open the door, they would fail the element. These data suggest a marked decrease in the ability to make correct decisions throughout the scenario.

PHYSIOLOGICAL RESPONSE TO STRESS

A primary focus of this study was to examine the response(s) of the body to stress. One of the unique aspects of the body's reactivity to stress is as Hans Selye described, the "general" adaptation that takes place. Indeed, the body has the same automatic response whether it is faced with a cold temperature, physical trauma, lack of oxygen, a difficult written exam, or a physical confrontation. These situations or stressors are diverse, but the response of the body can be the same. The sympathetic nervous system immediately activates numerous body systems to prepare for the fight or flight response. Two major body functions, heart rate (HR) and blood pressure, are elevated quickly during time of stress and fortunately, are easy to monitor. The second physiological system to respond to stress and complement the nervous system is the endocrine system. Providing a slower yet more prolonged response, the endocrine system releases chemicals throughout the body that intensify and sustain most of the neural actions that are already responding to the stressful stimulus.

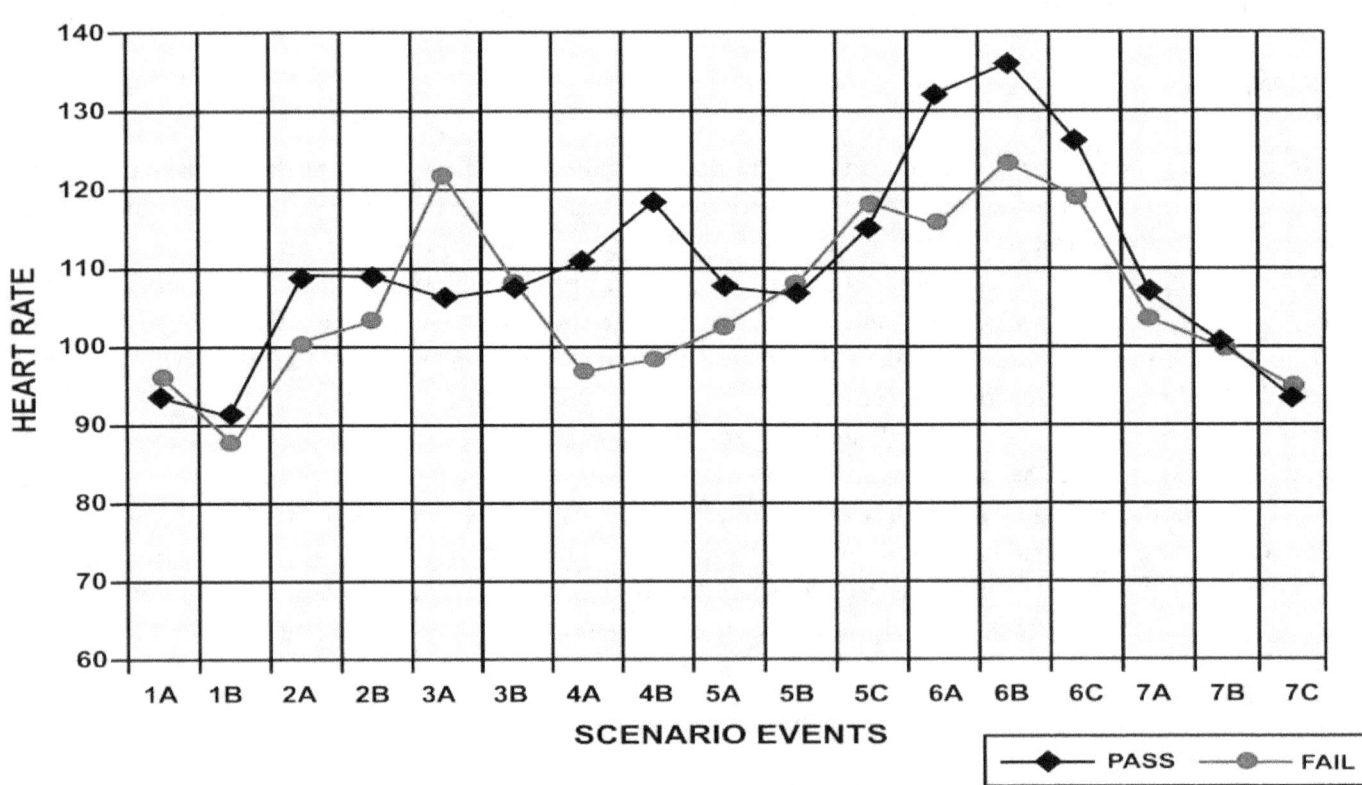

COMPARISON OF TRAINEE PERFORMANCE (PASS VS FAIL) BY HEART RATE

Heart Rate

As anticipated, HR was significantly elevated throughout the research scenario. HR data was used to address three research questions:

> Can we validate our training scenarios as being realistic/highly stressful?

> Can specific physiological factors be identified that predict performance in a highly stressful law enforcement encounter?

> Can specific physiological factors be used to identify an "optimum stress level for optimum performance" as suggested by various authors?

The HR values did replicate values and patterns noted in comparable stress studies, although a slightly higher HR was anticipated. The scenario was described (especially the shooting portion) as highly stressful by the participants; however, it did not produce HR values that were comparable in intensity. Changes in other physiological components served to support participants' assertions that the scenario was stressful.

The previous chart also addresses the question whether HR may serve as a predictor of successful versus unsuccessful performance of law enforcement activities. As reflected in the chart, there was little difference in HR between those that passed and those that failed the seven events. Significant differences between the pass / fail groups were noted only at periods 4a, 4b, and 6a. As these brief periods of difference were not sustained during the scenario, it does not appear that they play a key role in determining successful performance of law enforcement activities.

The HR values also provided important data related to another issue that was mentioned earlier in this paper, that of the moderate effects of stress in an "inverted U" pattern. During the shooting portion of the scenario, trainees exhibited HR's that should have put them at an optimum stress level (if HR does indeed accurately reflect the level of stress). The trainees did not, however, demonstrate optimum performance in this phase. One explanation is that, although HR is influenced by stress, its rise is not necessarily proportionate to the intensity of the stress, and is not a precise gauge of stress intensity.

Blood Pressure

Blood pressure readings throughout the scenario also indicated the increasing demand on the CNS. The systolic blood pressure (SBP) values were significantly elevated throughout the scenario, reaching an average value of 169 mm Hg during event 6a and 6b with a similar increase in 5c. As the interaction escalated between the student and the role players, so did the SBP value.

When comparing SBP between passing and non-passing students in each event, there was no noticeable difference. Systolic blood pressure frequently provides a valid indication of stress and its magnitude as demonstrated

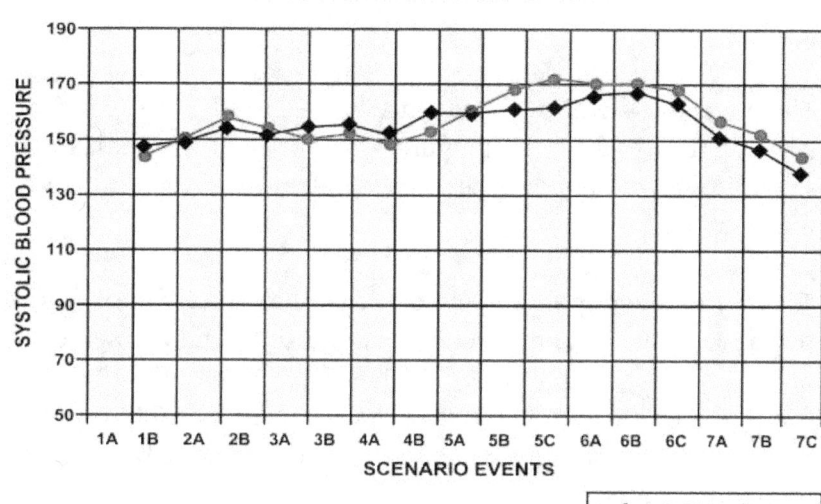

COMPARISON OF TRAINEE PERFORMANCE (PASS VS FAIL) BY SYSTOLIC BLOOD PRESSURE

34

by the numerous studies that use this value to monitor reactivity in the subject. In this study, the passing students demonstrated a similar degree of reactivity as the non-passing students.

As expected, the diastolic blood pressure (DBP) values changed relatively little during the scenario. Although there were some sizeable changes in specific students, the average values changed very little for the group. A moderate rise took place during event 5 when the officers made contact with the complainant and there was the gradual escalation of interaction between individuals. Both SBP and DBP results formed response patterns consistent with related literature. The magnitude of SBP elevation supported the research question of stress intensity and realism. The magnitude of increase more closely patterns that shown in the literature and may well be a better gauge of stress intensity than heart rate – although this study did not attempt to prove it as such.

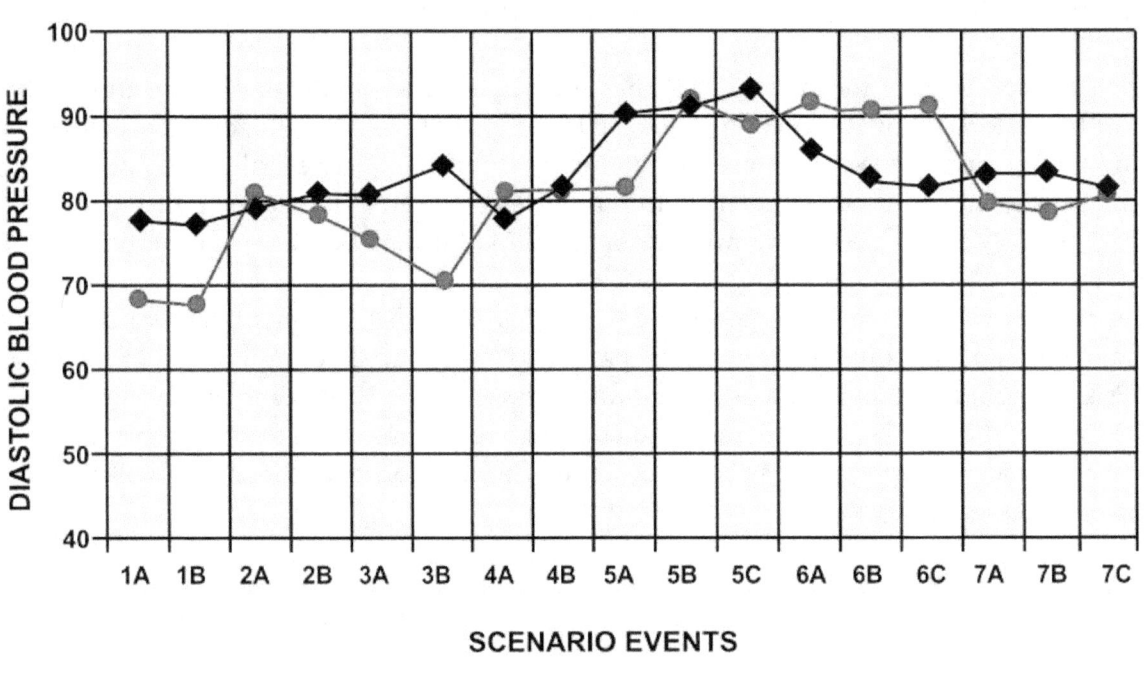

COMPARISON OF TRAINEE PERFORMANCE (PASS VS FAIL) BY DIASTOLIC BLOOD PRESSURE

There was one significant difference between DBP values for the passing versus the non-passing students; occurring in event 6c. Due to the intermingling course of the DBP values between the students that performed satisfactorily and those students who did not, it appears that DBP provides very little indication of which students will perform satisfactorily in the scenario.

To compare the response of these three cardiovascular measures, they have been displayed in the same graph. The rapid response of the HR and systolic blood pressure can be observed in the early phases of the research scenario.

It is interesting to note the rapid elevation of HR and SBP at the onset of the scenario while DBP is virtually unchanged. The SBP and HR tend to mirror each other throughout the scenario and provide confirmation of the reactivity of the stress response.

COMPARISON OF THE CARDIOVASCULAR MEASURES:
HEART RATE, SYSTOLIC AND DIASTOLIC BLOOD PRESSURE

Legend: ●— HEART RATE   ◆— SYSTOLIC BLOOD PRESSURE   ■— DIASTOLIC BLOOD PRESSURE

(X-axis: BASE LINE, 1A, 1B, 2A, 2B, 3A, 3B, 4A, 4B, 5A, 5B, 5C, 6A, 6B, 6C, 7A, 7B, 7C, POST. Y-axis: 0 to 180)

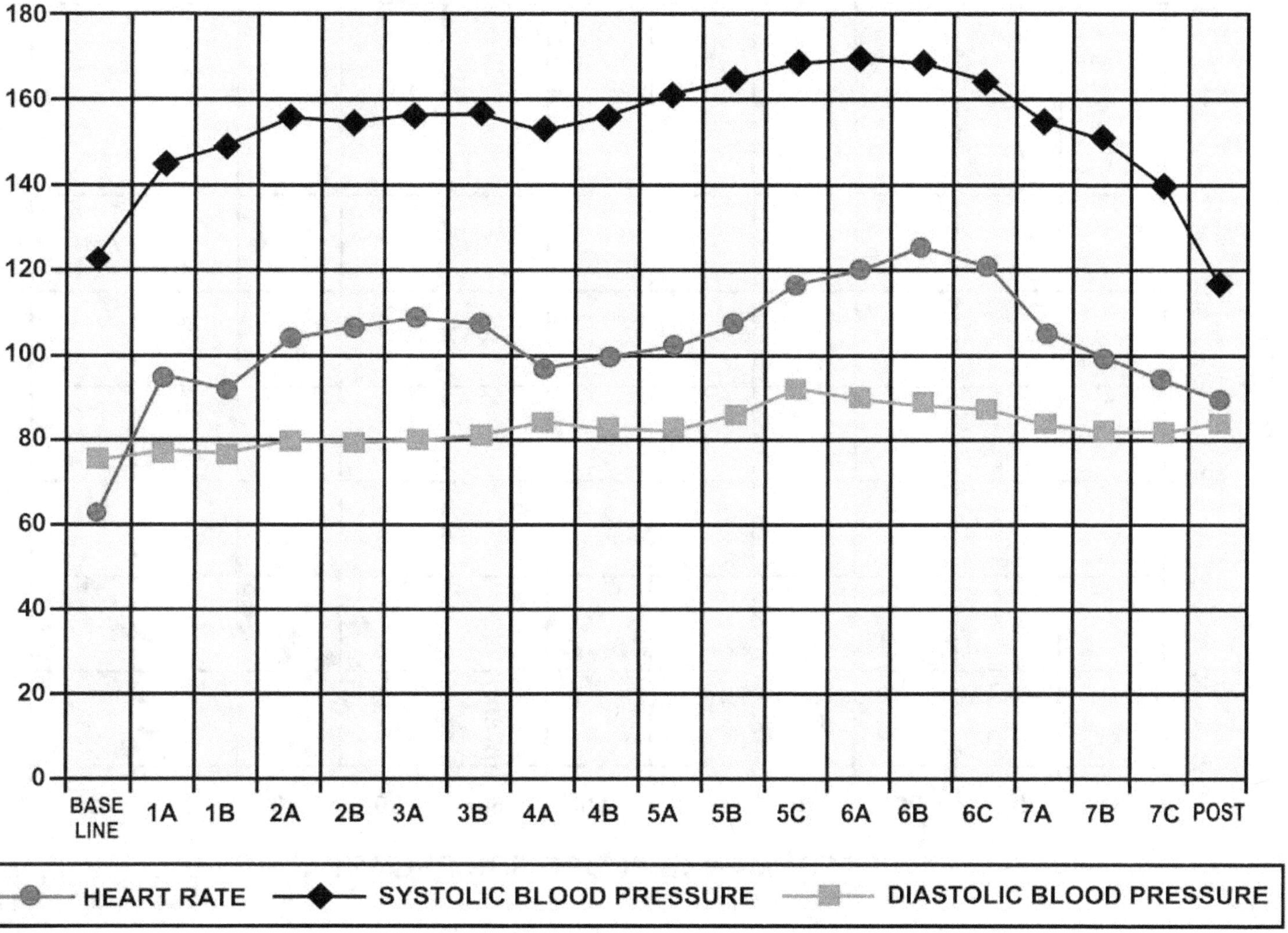

Cortisol

Cortisol levels (one of the primary indicators of the stress response), rose significantly during the scenario as illustrated in the following chart.

The cortisol levels compare favorably to those reported in other research studies using psychologically induced stress to actuate the neuro-chemical stress response. Due to method of collection (saliva), samples could only be taken at specific and limited times during the scenario as opposed to the repeated cardiovascular measures of HR, SBP, and DBP.

The four collection periods are reflected in the this chart. A comparison of the cortisol values between students receiving passing versus non-passing scores is presented in the next chart.

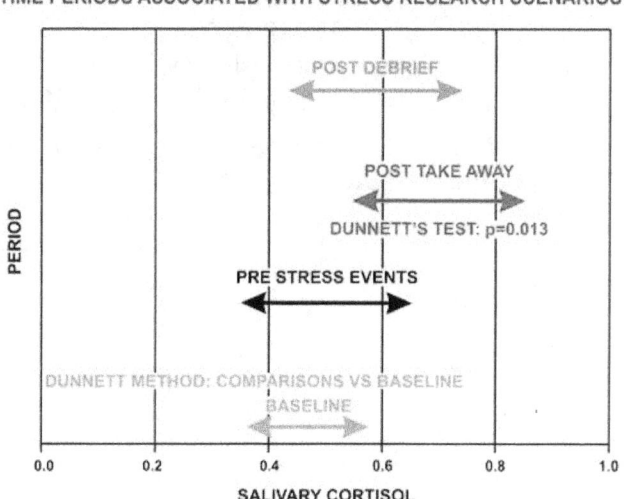

95%CONFIDENCE INTERVALS FOR SALIVARY CORTISOL BY TIME PERIODS ASSOCIATED WITH STRESS RESEARCH SCENARIOS

POST DEBRIEF

POST TAKE AWAY

DUNNETT'S TEST: p=0.013

PRE STRESS EVENTS

DUNNETT METHOD: COMPARISONS VS BASELINE

BASELINE

PERIOD

SALIVARY CORTISOL

COMPARISON OF TRAINEE PERFORMANCE (PASS VS FAIL) BY CORTISOL VALUES

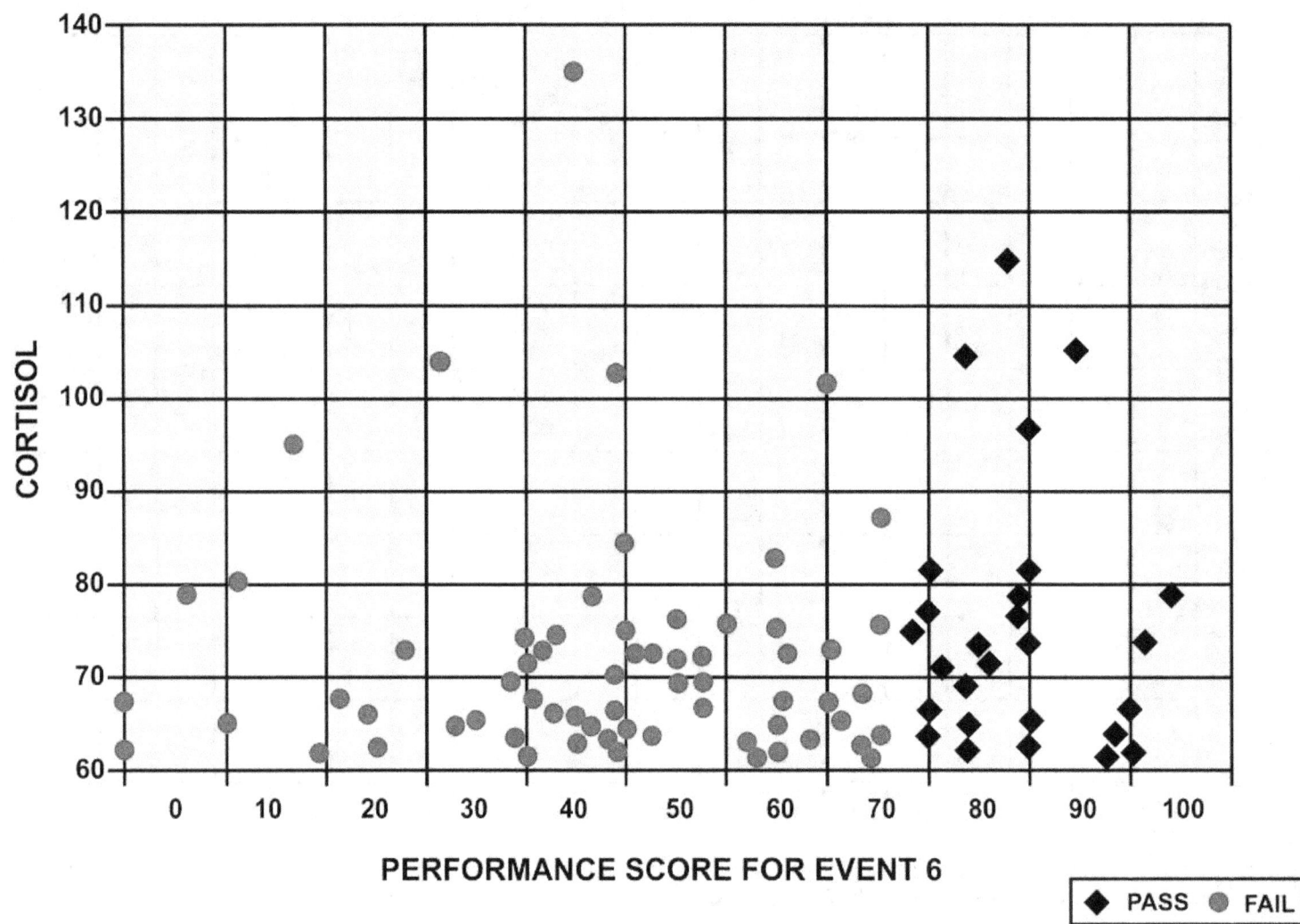

This chart compares cortisol level and performance during event 6 which included the gun takeaway and exchange of shooting. The even distribution of scores indicates that cortisol levels provide no information concerning how successful a student will be in this stressful encounter. Similar to the previously described factors, the change in cortisol verified that the scenario was an emotionally challenging one. Salivary cortisol provided a secondary method of verification (using the endocrine versus nervous system) and it was easy to collect samples without altering the flow of the scenario.

Future Research and Training Implications

The collection of physiological data allowed the research team to verify that the law enforcement scenario was indeed emotionally stressful, and afforded the subjects the opportunity to demonstrate their proficiency in responding under stressful conditions. While significant increases in heart rate, systolic blood pressure, and cortisol were documented throughout the scenario, there were essentially no relationships among the variables and effective performance. One explanation commonly cited in other studies is that the stress response is so highly individualized that highly reactive individuals (high heart rate and blood pressure) may perform calmly and proficiently, but a subject with a minimal stress response may make numerous errors and perform poorly. These factors indicate that the individual is undergoing a stressful situation, but they do not indicate if that level of stress is high, low, or somewhere in between. The results of this study generally support such a hypothesis.

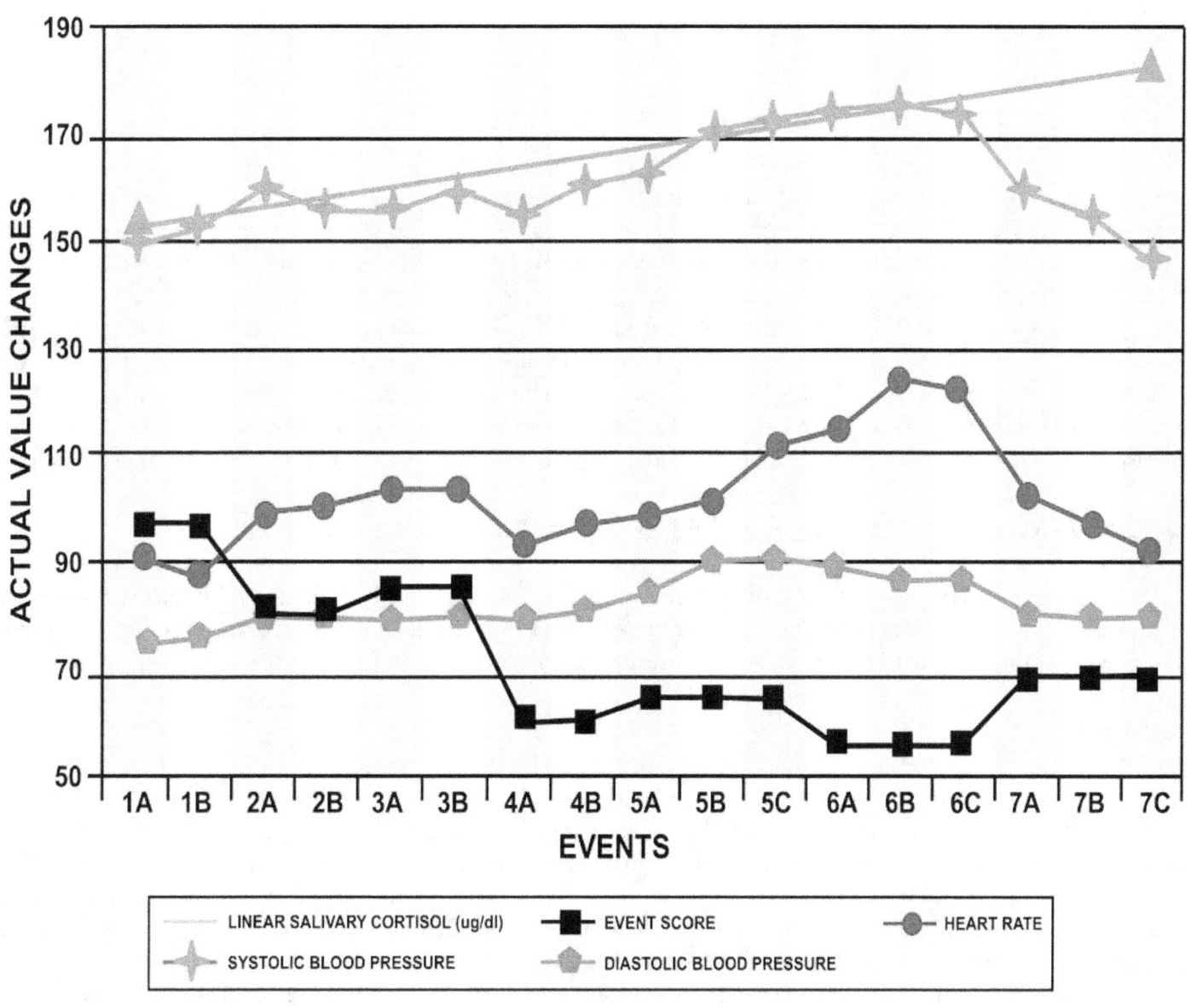

Graph 2 depicts actual values for each phase of the seven events. This graph more accurately depicts the individual variances found at the moments selected for data analysis than the linear trend lines.

In light of these findings, it would be inaccurate to state, for example, that a specific heart rate or systolic blood pressure value places an individual in (or out of) a high stress zone. A zone or performance level where the amount of stress dictates perceptual and cognitive narrowing (the brain begins to limit input and mental processing) is unique to each individual and cannot be structured into a precise zone. It was also observed that decision-making skills appeared to be hindered when heart rate levels were elevated (through psychological/emotional stress) to levels of 110 and 120 beats per minute (bpm). The value of 110 bpm is not a precise threshold, but is identified here to suggest that cognitive narrowing can take place without a 150 heart rate or SBP of 170. Additionally, the limited mental processing was induced through emotional rather than physical means. Due to a difference in triggering mechanisms (neuromuscular stress or exercise versus emotional stress) the mental processing capacity is far different. **It would be erroneous to use physical activity alone to elevate heart rate and blood pressure in order to simulate a highly stressful "psychological" encounter. Training under conditions of psychological/ emotional stress will better prepare the brain to perform under those conditions when the need arises.** A heart rate of 140 induced by exercise is quite common for joggers and rarely impairs their mental processing. If that same heart rate is obtained through emotional stress, the decision making ability of the individual would most likely be impaired. **The importance is in the *process* of how the stress is created, rather than in the *product* of how the stress is measured.**

PSYCHOLOGICAL RESPONSE TO STRESS

One of the first analyses performed was to determine if the volunteers accurately reflected the other members of the basic training program. The volunteers did indeed possess a profile similar to their peers with slightly higher scores for state and trait curiosity and lower scores for state and trait anxiety. For all general purposes, the volunteers were similar to the non volunteers, and the two training programs were not significantly different

The results of general administration of the STPI and STAXI instruments suggest that the volunteers for this stress research study are slightly more curious than those who did not volunteer and compared to national norms, view themselves as being less anxious during various situations. This suggests that the effects of stress on a different research population may very well have produced a greater stress response; however, this was a law enforcement scenario developed for law enforcement personnel and caution should be used when making any generalizations.

STPI and STAXI State and Trait scales and Physiological Data

A Pearson correlation coefficient and stepwise regression analysis were used to identify physiological predictors of performance during the scenario. The Trait and Anger values were compared to heart rate, systolic and diastolic blood pressure values recorded during each of the seven scenario events, and the post-scenario cortisol sample.

Heart Rate

Pearson Correlation Coefficients were calculated for heart rate (17 measurements) and the nine Trait/Anger and four State scales. A significant correlation was found ($\alpha = .05$) for seven different Trait/Anger scales and three different State scales. Anger In was the most frequent scale in which significant correlations were found (eleven). Trait Curiosity and State Anxiety were second and third with six and five significant correlations respectively. A stepwise regression analysis was performed comparing heart rate to the identified scales. Significant Trait/Anger and State scale predictors were found ($\alpha = .05$) for fourteen of the seventeen measurements of heart rate. Anger In was the most frequent scale in which significant correlations were found (eight). State Anxiety and State Curiosity each had four significant coefficients in the prediction equation.

Systolic Blood Pressure

Pearson Correlation Coefficients were calculated for systolic blood pressure (17 measurements) and the nine Trait/Anger and four State scales. Weak but statistically significant correlations were found ($\alpha = .05$) for eight different Trait/Anger scales and two different State scales. State Curiosity was the most frequent scale with eight significant correlations. State Depression and Trait Curiosity were second and third with six and five significant correlations respectively. A stepwise regression analysis was performed comparing systolic values to the identified scales. State Curiosity was the most frequent scale with six significant coefficients in the prediction equation. State Depression and Trait Curiosity were second and third with three and two significant occurrences in the prediction equation. Three of the systolic blood pressure measures had multiple significant Trait/Anger and State scale predictors.

Diastolic Blood Pressure

Pearson Correlation Coefficients were calculated for diastolic blood pressure (17 measurements) and the nine Trait/Anger and four State scales. Weak but statistically significant correlations were found ($\alpha = .05$) for seven different Trait/Anger scales and three different State scales. State Curiosity, Trait Curiosity, and Control Out were the most frequent scales with five significant correlations each. A stepwise regression analysis was performed comparing diastolic values to the identified scales. Significant Trait/Anger and State scale relationships were found ($\alpha = .05$) for seven of the seventeen measurements of diastolic blood pressure. State Curiosity was the most frequent scale with three significant occurrences in the prediction equation. Trait Curiosity was second with two significant coefficients in the prediction equation. One of the diastolic blood pressure measures had multiple significant Trait/Anger and State scale coefficients used in the prediction equation.

Immediate Post Cortisol

A Pearson Correlation Coefficient was performed comparing the subject's immediate- post cortisol level, the nine Trait/Anger, and four State scales. No significant correlations were found. A stepwise regression analysis was conducted between the subject's immediate- post cortisol level, the nine Trait/Anger, and four State scales. No significant Trait/Anger and State scale predictors were found ($\alpha = .05$) for subject's immediate- post cortisol level.

Implications of STPI / STAXI to Physiological Factors

Comparison of the measures of heart rate, systolic and diastolic blood pressure to the trait/anger and state scales indicates that there are numerous correlations that can be termed "statistically significant." The findings associated with the stepwise regression analysis indicate that selected STPI and STAXI variables can be used to detect relationships between physiological and psychological measures in the context of this study. Anger In was the most frequently related scale with heart rate obtaining statistical significance on eight of the seventeen comparisons. State and Trait Curiosity scores show a relationship to numerous systolic blood pressure readings throughout the scenario. Although these relationships are termed "significant", the strength of these relationships is minimal and their usefulness unclear ($p< 0.1$ to 0.3). Understanding that "correlation does establish causation," these minimal relationships need to be further explored. There does appear to be some relationship between psychological states and traits and the physiological measures in this study. The indistinct impact of these relationships is further blurred in light of the minimal impact the physiological factors had in determining successful from unsuccessful performance in the research scenario.

Event 6 Score

A Pearson Correlation Coefficient was performed comparing the subjects' average Event 6 score, the nine Trait/Anger, and four State scales. Significant correlations (.195) were found ($\alpha = .04$) for Trait Anger, for Anger Out (.196) and ($\alpha = .039$), and for Anger Index (.209) and ($\alpha = .029$). No significant Trait/Anger and State scale predictors were found ($\alpha = .05$) for the subjects' Event 6 score in the stepwise regression analysis.

Shot Placement Score

Significant correlations (.268) were found ($\alpha = .009$) for Trait Anger and for Anger Out (.200) and ($\alpha = .041$) using the Pearson Correlation Coefficient. Trait Anger was the only significant Trait/Anger and State scale predictor found ($\alpha = .05$) for the subjects' shot placement score using a stepwise regression analysis.

Overall Scenario Score

Trait Anger was the only scale with a statistically significant correlation of (.318) ($\alpha = .002$). Trait Anger was the only significant Trait/Anger and State scale predictor found ($\alpha = .05$) using the stepwise regression analysis.

Cognitive Score

Significant correlations (.267) ($\alpha = .008$) were found for Trait Curiosity, Trait Anger (.248) ($\alpha = .012$), Anger Out (.211) ($\alpha = .029$), and Anger Index (.216) ($\alpha = .026$). Trait Curiosity was the most significant Trait/Anger and State scale predictor for the subjects' cognitive score.

Implications for training and future research

The comparison of the measures of subject performance and the trait/anger and state scales indicates that there are statistical relationships between these variables. Trait/Anger scales generally demonstrated a higher correlation than the State scales. Even with the four state variables being significantly elevated during the scenario; State Anxiety 93rd percentile, State Anger 79th percentile, State Depression 71 percentile, and State Curiosity 70th percentile, little was provided in terms of predicting performance during the scenario. The components of Anger-In (the frequency angry feelings are experienced but not expressed) and Trait Anger showed a relationship to the scenario firearms score and shot placement along with the overall scenario score. While taking into consideration the conservative baseline scores, these low to moderate correlations may take on greater significance with further testing.

A final word of caution about the interpretation of these results is in order. These are complex relationships and how they interact will remain unclear without further research. Unintended trade-offs in performance could result from the premature application of some of these weak predictor coefficients to training.

DISCUSSION OF RESULTS

High-risk law enforcement scenarios often develop suddenly and unpredictably from a situation initially appearing as routine. They demand a high level of cognitive skills for successful outcomes, in addition to a high level of training. Cognitive responses are required, such as assessment of the situation, identification of "friend or foe," coordinating actions with other officers and dispatcher, and giving appropriate commands, as well as the decision on the use of force. The urgency and complexity of such situations are challenging mentally, emotionally, and physically.

An assessment paradigm was created; selecting tasks exclusively from specific training previously provided the students. A subset of critical tasks was integrated into a fast-flowing, realistic scenario in such a way as to allow the measurement of several cognitive, physiological (stress indices) and psychological responses, as well as performance scores, at frequent time intervals. Performance attributes, which were assessed, included: emergency vehicle operation, perception of surroundings (presence of innocent civilians, availability of cover), threat assessment, appropriate level of use of force, verbal communications, firearms skills, as well as post-event ability to recall and describe actions. This paradigm would allow us to collect and evaluate subject responses longitudinally, either alone or in combination with each other in multivariate models. Moreover, the succession of settings with varying "demand loads" and "cues" would allow evaluation of multiple factors and their reciprocal relationship to physiological responses. The research scenario was designed to quantify the stressfulness of the paradigm, determine the effect of stress on cognitive abilities and performance, examine the relationship of psychological and physiological indicators to performance, and identify areas of the training which may benefit from the results of this study.

The FLETC is committed to seeking new and better ways to deliver effective training to students in Federal officer and agent programs. This research scenario provided a format to ensure that our training programs are realistic and challenging, without exceeding students' capabilities. FLETC is also committed to increasing awareness of the effects of stress on performance, as part of the training for survival of the officers and agents. Rather than merely providing students with specific skills of the profession, we must challenge them to be able to select appropriate responses as required, integrating them into performance that remains resilient and effective in stressful, fast-moving real-life incidents. Such highly fluid situations demand continuous, accurate threat assessment and changing tactics. This capacity is most critical in hose situations that rapidly escalate into crises in which life or death depends upon instantaneous and appropriate responses.

Discussion of Research Questions

The objective of this research was to develop a "Survival Score Index" and to answer the following key research questions:

> **1. Can we validate our training scenarios as being realistic/highly stressful? Trainees are asked to perform law enforcement skills in scenarios that replicate real world situations that are stressful. This component will compare the stress response of trainees in this study to the stress response measured in other studies designed to elicit an acute stress response.**

The results previously identified in this study indicate that law enforcement training scenarios of this nature are indeed realistic and highly stressful. Law enforcement scenarios are particularly mentally and emotionally demanding, and require training that addresses these unique demands. High stress training is required to expose trainees to these conditions in order that they are prepared to respond effectively in the field. The degradation in cognitive skills (which in turn impairs performance) was demonstrated throughout the research study. It is the belief of the research team that performance levels can be improved through a greater exposure to high stress training.

2. Can specific psychological factors be identified that predict performance in a highly stressful law enforcement encounter?

The relationship of psychological factors to performance in a high stress encounter will require further examination. Trait Anger is of special interest with significant correlations found in Event 6 (Gun take-away and shooting), shot placement score, cognitive score, and overall scenario score. The Anger Index and Anger Out values were also present in several critical areas along with Curiosity. These relationships require closer review to explore their significance to responding in a stressful environment as well as how this information would be used to improve training.

3. Can specific physiological factors be identified that predict performance in a highly stressful law enforcement encounter?

One of the more notable findings of this study was that physiological factors do indeed respond to this type of stressful encounter, but not precisely in the manner that was anticipated. Although heart rate does elevate with emotional stress, it did not increase to the extent we had believed it would. Not only was the general range of heart rate responses lower than projected, but the range of increase had no relationship to satisfactory and unsatisfactory performance. The degree of increase in heart rate was unique to each individual and was not a limiting factor for mental or physical performance. Heart rate guided training has been promoted by several programs as the preferred method of choice for replicating high emotional stress. This study did not support that premise and showed that the stress zone (as measured by heart rate) is much lower. Additionally, even when heart rate is monitored, it provided no indication / predictability of successful performance. Low heart rates had the same pass/fail rate as high heart rates. Systolic blood pressure values more closely resembled the magnitude of increase previously reported in literature. Systolic values, nevertheless, had no predictive capacity in differentiating between satisfactory and unsatisfactory performance.

4. Can specific physiological factors be used to identify an "optimum stress level for optimum performance" as suggested by various authors?

Within the parameters of this study, there appeared to be no optimum zone of performance. When measured by heart rate, there was no difference in success rates for trainee who had heart rates in the low, middle, or upper portions of their heart rate zones. The "zone of optimum performance" where individuals perform at their best may very well be identified through mental/emotional assessments, but are not identified at a precise heart rate, blood pressure, or cortisol level physiologically. It was the mental/emotional stress that generated the perceptual and cognitive narrowing (hence the psychological, emotional, and physiological stress) found in this study. Occasionally, trainers use conditioning or fitness induced stress to elevate the heart rate and blood to simulate a stressful environment.

Due to a difference in triggering mechanisms (exercise versus emotional stress), the cognitive/ mental processing capacity is far different. The acute stress scenario used in the study requires the cerebrum to analyze thousands of pieces of information in order to respond to numerous unknown situations. It is the brain's perception of a potential threat and activation to the "fight or flight stress response" that triggers the increased heart rate and blood pressure. In fitness induced stress, the "perceived" threat is known - - it is the challenge of lifting a certain weight or running at a specific pace . When individuals run, heart rate and blood pressure respond automatically. It is the exercise dictating the cardiovascular response, as opposed to the emotions triggering the cardiovascular response as observed in the research scenario. It would be erroneous to use physical activity solely as a stimulus to elevate heart rate and blood pressure order to simulate a highly stressful "psychological" encounter. Training under psychological/emotional stress will better prepare the brain to perform under those conditions when the need arises versus having trainees exercise. The focus should be in the process of how the stress is created (the stimulus), rather than in the product of how the stress is measured (the response).

5. What effect does high stress have on decision-making (cognitive processing)?

This project provided repeated and measured examples of perceptual narrowing, poor decision-making skills, low cognitive scores, the reduced ability to perform sequential motor skills, and diminished recall of events during high stress. Decisions to not use the radio or verbal commands, maintain position of advantage while under fire, and to shoot at inappropriate times were cognitive decisions that produced notably poor performance. Manual skills such as reload failures, improper clearing of the weapon and operation of the radio were physical skills negatively impacted by the cognitive process. These findings support previous research as to the negative effects of stress on decision-making and on performance.

As identified in the research design, one of the goals of this project was to identify elements of the stress response that could be used to develop a "survival score index" to assist trainers in assessing performance in a stressful training environment. This project has made significant contributions towards achieving that goal. Identifiable law enforcement skills were isolated and evaluated within the data set. While no scoring system will be developed at this stage, this work will serve as a foundation for knowledge of the stress effect in a law enforcement situation. Further research will need to be conducted to test corrective training practices that will offset observed deficiencies in performance.

RECOMMENDATIONS

Over 368 variables were examined in this research study which has spanned two years. The amount of data collected is as overwhelming as it is impressive. The team has analyzed only a fraction of the data that potentially could be rendered in a research project this size and only a small portion of the analyzed data have been presented in this abbreviated report. These recommendations are based on the overall analyses, with limited focus on areas of immediate concern.

Additional analysis by subject-matter experts

Further analysis could, and should be conducted with this data set. It is recommended teams be established to more closely analyze the data and perhaps conduct further analysis of the data set in order to make decisions as to the need for change or additional research. Potential areas to be examined more closely include but are not limited to: communications, firearms sequencing skills, weapons handling skills, tactical retreat, and use of force.

Increase scenario-based training

A review of the literature indicates students need experiences to draw upon when rendering decisions. Students without such experiences have difficulty making the leap in applying knowledge learned in one environment to another area. Examples of this are seen daily by FLETC training staff as trainees report inconsistencies in training that are, in fact, the students inability to transfer the knowledge to a different set of conditions. The best way to develop these experiences is through practice in a scenario exercise. It therefore recommended trainers consider additional scenario training.

Scenario training should be stressful in nature. Creating memories of effective actions while under stress allows the trainee to more quickly implement appropriate actions in similar stressful situations. Proper preparation of the student for potential outcomes of their performance under stress can also add to the training benefit of training under stress. The student will become better aware of his or her own capabilities under stress.

Phase II of this project be approved and funded

Phase II of this project is designed to continue to focus on the goal of identifying performance indicators that lend itself to a survival score. Areas were identified that will lay the foundation for focusing on the establishment of actual survival scores in law enforcement training. This next phase includes the analysis of this data set for indicators of stress and performance as well as sequencing training through stressful scenarios and recovery times essential for optimum performance.

BIBLIOGRAPHY

Asterita, M.F. (1985). The physiology of stress. New York: Human Science Press, Inc.

Baumgartner, A., Graf, K-J., & Kurten, I. (1985). The dexamathasone suppression test in depression, in schizophrenia and during experimental stress. Biol. Psychiatry 20:675-679.

Biaggio, M.K., Supplee, K. & Curtis, N. (1981). Reliability and validity of four anger scales. Journal of Personality Assessments, 45, 639-648.

Brown, J.,& Campbell, E. (1994). Stress and Policing: Sources and Strategies. John Wiley & Sons, Chichester.

Buono, M..J., Yeager, J.E. & Hodgdon, J.A. (1986) Plasma adrenocorticotropin and cortisol responses to brief high-intensity exercise in humans. Journal of Applied Physiology 61(4): 1337-1339.
Carter, R. (1999). Mapping the mind. Berkley: University of California Press.

Cannon, W. B. (1915, 1989). Bodily changes in pain, hunger, fear and rage; an account of recent researches into the function of emotional excitement. Birmingham: Classics of Psychiatry.

Cannon, W. B. (1929). Bodily changes in pain, hunger, fear and rage. Appleton, New York.

Chatterton, R.T., Vogelsong, K.M., Lu, Y-C., Ellman, A.B., & Hudgens, G.A. (1996). Salivary-amylase as a measure of endogenous adrenergic activity. Clinical Physiology 16, 433-448.

Corenblum, B., & Taylor, P.J. (1981). Mechanisms of control of prolactin release in response to apprehension stress and anesthesia-surgery stress. Fertility and Sterility 36(6): 712-715.

Czeisler C.A., Moore-Ede M.C., Regestein Q.R., Kisch E.S., Fang V.S. & Ehrlich E.N.(1976). Episodic 24-hour cortisol secretory patterns in patients awaiting elective cardiac surgery. J. Clin. Endo. Metabolism 42(2): 273-283.

Damsasio, A.R. (1994). Descartes' error: emotion, reason and the human brain. Avon books Hearst, New York.
Dato, Robert (1978). The law of stress, Stress, Vol. 3, No.1.

Darwin, C. (1965). The expression of emotions in man and animals. Chicago: University of Chicago Press. (Originally published 1872)

Darwin, C. R. Microsoft® Encarta® Online Encyclopedia 2002 http://encarta.msn.com (9 May. 2002).

de Kloet, E. R., Oitzl, M. S., and Joels, M. (1999) Stress and cognition: are corticosteroids good or bad guys? Viewpoint Vol. 22 No. 10)pp. 422-426)

DeQuervain DJ-F, Roozendall, B. & McLaugh, J. (1998). Stress and glucocorticoids impair retrieval of long-term spatial memory. Nature, 394:787-790.

DeQuervain DJ-F, Roozendall, B., Nitsch, R., McGaugh, J. & Hock, C. (2000) Acute cortisone administration impairs retrieval of long-term declarative memory in humans. Nature Neuroscience, 394:313-314.

Dimsdale, J.E. & Moss, J. (1980). Short-term catecholamine response to psychological stress. Psychosomatic Medicine 42(5): 493-497,.

Deuster, P., Chrousos, G., Luger, A., DeBolt, J., Bernier, L., Trostmann, U., Kyle, S., Montgomery, L. & Loriaux, D. (1989). Hormonal and metabolic responses of untrained, moderately trained, and highly trained men to three exercise intensities. Metabolism. 38(2):141-148.

Driskell, J. E., & Salas, E. (1991). Overcoming the effects of stress on military performance: Human factors, training, and selection strategies. I R. Gal & A. D. Mangelsdorf (Eds.) Handbook of Military Psychology. New York: Wiley.

Driskell, J. E., & Salas, E. (1996). Stress and human performance. Mahwah, New Jersey: Lawrence Erlbaum Associates, Inc.

Driskell, J. E., Johnston, J. H., & Salas, E. (1997). Vigilant and hypervigilant decision making. Journal of Applied Psychology, Vol. 82 No. 4, 614-622.

Eliot, R. S., & Breo, D. L. (1989). Is It Worth Dying For?: How to Make Stress Work For You-Not Against You. New York: Bantam Doubleday Dell Publishing Group.

Ely, D.L.& Mostardi, R.A.(1986). The effect of recent life events stress, life assets, and temperament pattern on cardiovascular risk factors for Akron City police officers. J. Human Stress 12(2), 77-91.

Federal Bureau of Investigations. (2000). FBI Uniform Crime Report 2000. [Online] Available http://www.fbi.gov/ucr/ucr.htm

Fenz, W.D. & Epstein, S. (1967). Gradients of physiological arousal in parachutists as a function of an approaching jump. Psychosom. Med. 29 (1), 33-51.

Fenz, W.D. & Jones, G.B. (1972). Individual differences in physiologic arousal and performance in sport parachutists. Psychosom. Med. 34 (1), 1-8.

Franke, W.D., Collins, S.A.& Hinz, P.N. (1998). Cardiovascular disease morbidity in an Iowa law enforcement cohort, compared with the general Iowa population. J. Occup Environ Med 40(5) 441-444.

Frankenhaeuser, M., Von Wright, M.R., Collins, A., Von Wright, J., Sedvall, G., & Swahn, C.G. (1978) Sex differences in psychoneuroendocrine reactions to examination stress. Psychosom. Med. 40(4): 334-343.

Friedman, M. and Rosenman, R. (1959). Association of a specific over behavior pattern with increases in blood cholesterol, in blood clotting time, incidence of arcus senilis and clinical coronary artery disease. J. Am. Med. Assoc. 169,1286-1296.

Glass, C.R., Arnkoff, D.B., Wood, H., Meyerhoff, J.L., Smith, H.R., Oleshansky, M.A., & Hedges, S. (1995). Cognition, anxiety and performance on a career-related oral examination. J. Counseling Psychol. 42 (1), 47-54.

Grinker, R.R., & Spiegel, J.P. (1945). Men under stress. Blakiston, Philadelphia.

Grossman, D., & Siddle, B. K. (1998). Critical incident amnesia: the physiological basis and the implications of memory loss during extreme survival stress situations. PPCT Management Systems, March.

Hanin, Y. L. (2000). Successful and poor performance and emotions. In Yuri L. Hanin (Ed.), Emotions in Sport (pp. 157-188). Champaign, Ill: Human Kinetics.

Hansen, J.H.L., C. Swail, A.J. South, R.K. Moore, H. Steeneken, E.J. Cupples, T. Anderson, C.R.A. Vloeberghs, I. Trancoso, & P. Verlinde (2000) The Impact of Speech Under `Stress' on Military Speech Technology published by NATO Research & Technology Organization RTO-TR-10, AC/323(IST)TP/5 IST/TG-01, March 2000 (ISBN: 92-837-1027-4).

Hanson, J.R., Stoa, K.F., Blix, A.S. & Ursin, H. (1978). Urinary levels of epinephrine and norepinephrine in parachutist trainees. In Ursin, H., Baade, E., Levine, S., (eds), Psychobiology of Stress: A Study of Coping Men. New York, Academic Press, New York, pp. 63-74.

Hartley, L.H., Mason, J.W., Hogan, R.P., Jones, L.G., Kotchen, T.A., Mougey, E.H., Wherry, F.E., Pennington, L.L.,& Ricketts, P.T. (1972). Multiple hormonal responses to graded exercise in relation to physical training. Journal of Applied Physiology 33(5): 602-606, 607-610.

HeartMath Research Center. (1999). Impact of HearthMath Self-Management Skills Program on Physiological and Psychological Stress in Police Officers. Boulder Creek, CA.

Hick, W.E. (1952). On the rate of Gain of Information. Quarterly Journal of Experimental Psychology # 4. (pp. 11-26).

Howard, P. J. (2000). The owner's manual for the brain. Austin, Texas: Bard Press.

Inzana, C. M., Driskell, J. E., Johnston, J. H., & Salas, E. (1996). Effects of preparatory information on enhancing performance under stress. Journal of Applied Psychology, Vol. 81 No. 4, 429-435.

Janis, I.L. and Mann, L. (1977). Decision Making: a psychological analysis of conflict, choice and commitment. New York: The Free Press.

Johnston, J. H. and Cannon-Bowers, J. A. (1996). Training for stress exposure. In J.E. Driskell & E. Salas (Eds.) Stress and human performance. Mahwah, New Jersey: Lawrence Erlbaum Associates, Inc.

Johnston, J.H., Smith-Jentsch, K. A., and Cannon-Bowers, J. A. (1997). Performance Measurement Tools for Enhancing Team Decision-Making Training. In. Brannick, M.T., Salas, E., and Prince, C. (Eds.) <u>Team Performance assessment and measurement: Theory, Methods, and applications.</u>. Hillsdale, NJ: LEA. (p. 313)

Johnston, J. H. et al (1997) Vigilant and Hypervigilant Decision Making. <u>Journal of Applied Psychology Vol 82, No. 4</u>, (pp 614-622).

Kagan, J. (1989). Temperamental contributions to social behavior. <u>American Psychologist</u>, 44, 668-674.

Kagan, J. (1989). <u>Unstable ideas: Temperament, cognition, and self</u>. Cambridge, MA: Harvard University Press.

Keinan, G. and Friedland, N. (1996). Training effective performance under stress: queries, dilemmas, and possible solutions. In J.E. Driskell & E. Salas (Eds.) <u>Stress and human performance.</u> Mahwah, New Jersey: Lawrence Erlbaum Associates, Inc.

Kirkcaldy, B., Cooper, & C.L., Ruffalo, P. (1995). Work stress and health in a sample of U.S. police. <u>Psychol Rep.</u> <u>76</u>(2) 700-702.

Kirschbaum, C., Read, G.F., & Hellhammer, D.H. (Eds.). (1992). <u>Assessment of hormones and drugs in saliva in biobehavioral research</u>. Hogrefe & Huber Publishers. Seattle.

Kirschbaum, C., Wolf, O., May, M., Wippich, W. and Hellhammer, D. (1996). Stress- and treatment-induced elevations of cortisol levels associated with impaired declarative memory in healthy adults. <u>Life Sciences 58</u>(17):1475-1483.

Kosinski, R.J. (2002). A Literature Review on Reaction Time. (On-line document) available http://biae.clemson.edu/bpc/bp/Lab/110/reaction.htm.

Lachar, B. L. (1993). Coronary Prone Behavior. <u>Texas Heart Institute Journal</u>, 20: 143-51.

Lake, C.R., Ziegler, M.G., & Kopin, I.J. (1976). Use of plasma norepinephrine for evaluation of sympathetic neuronal function in man. <u>Life Sciences 18</u>, 1315-1326.

Lazarus, R.S., & Folkman, S. (1984). <u>Stress, appraisal, and coping</u>. New York: Springer.

Lazarus, R.S., & Opton, F.M., Jr. (1966). The study of psychological stress. In C.D. Spielberger (Ed.), <u>Anxiety and behavior</u> (pp. 225-262). New York: Academic Press.

LeDoux, J. E. (1996). The emotional brain<u>: the emotional underpinnings of emotional life</u>. New York. Simon & Schuster Inc.

LeDoux, J. E. (2002). <u>Synaptic self: how our brains become who we are</u>. New York. Penguin Putnam Inc.

Levine, S. Cortisol changes following repeated experiences with parachute training. (1978). In Ursin, H., Baade, E., Levine, S. (eds), <u>Psychobiology of Stress: A Study of Coping Men</u>. New York, Academic Press, New York.

Lovallo, W.R., Pincomb, G.A., Edwards, G.A., Brackett, D.J.and Wilson, M.F. (1986). Work pressure and the type A behavior pattern exam stress in male medical students. <u>Psychosom. Med. 48</u>(1/2): 125-133.

Luger, A., Deuster, P.A., Kyle, S.B., Gallucci, W.T., Montgomery, L.C., Gold, P.W., Loriaux, D.L., and Chrousos, G.P. (1987). Acute hypothalamic-pituitary-adrenal responses to the stress of treadmill exercise: physiologic adaptations to physical training. <u>New Eng. J. Med., 316</u>:1309-1315.

Lupien, S and McEwen, B. (1997). The acute effects of corticosteroids on cognition: integration of animal and human studies. <u>Brain Research Reviews 24</u>:1-27.

Mason, L. J. (1985). <u>Guide to stress reduction.</u> Berkeley: Celestial Arts.

Mason, J.W. (1968). Over-all hormonal balance as a key to endocrine organization. Psychosomatic Medicine 30: 791-808.

Mearns, J.and Mauch, T.G.(1998). Negative mood regulation expectancies predict anger among police officers and buffer the effects of job stress. <u>J. Nerv Ment Dis. 186</u>(2) 120-125.

Meyerhoff, J. L., Oleshansky, M.A,, & Mougey, E.H. (1998). Psychological stress increases plasma levels of prolactin, cortisol and POMC-derived peptides in man. <u>Psychosom. Med. 50 (3),</u> 295-303.

Meyerhoff, J. L., Oleshansky, M. A., Kalogeras, K. T., Mougey, E. H., Chrousos, G. P., & Granger, L.G. (1990). Responses to emotional stress: possible interactions between circulating factors and anterior pituitary hormone release. In J.C. Porter & D. Jezova, (eds.) <u>Circulating Regulatory Factors and Neuroendocrine Function: Advances in Experimental Biology and Medicine.</u> (pp. 91-111). New York:Plenum Press.

Meyerhoff, J.L., M.A. Hebert, K.L. Huhman, E.H. Mougey, M.A.Oleshansky, M. Potegal, G.A. Saviolakis, D.L.Yourick and B.N. Bunnell. (2000) Operational stress and combat stress reaction: neurobiological approaches towards improving assessment of risk and enhancing intervention. In Karl Friedl, Harris Lieberman, Donna Ryan and George Bray (eds). <u>Countermeasures for Battlefield Stressors; Pennington Nutrition Series, vol. 10</u> Baton Rouge: Louisiana University Press.

Moss, A.J.and Wynar, B. (1970) Tachycardia in house officers presenting cases at grand rounds. <u>Annals of Internal Medicine 72</u>(2): 255-256.

Nesse, R.M., Curtis, G.C., Thyer, B.A., McCann, D.S., Huber-Smith, M.J.and Knopf, R.F. (1985). Endocrine and cardiovascular responses during phobic anxiety. <u>Psychosomatic Medicine 47</u>(1): 320-332.

Nexo, E., Hansen, M.R. and Konradsen, L. (1988). Human salivary epidermal growth factor, haptocorrin and amylase before and after prolonged exercise. <u>Scand. J. Clin. Lab. Invest.</u> 48:269-273.

Noel, G.L., Dimond, R.C., Earll, J.M.and Frantz, A.G. (1976) Prolactin, thyrotropin, and growth hormone release during stress associated with parachute jumping. Aviation, Space and Environmental Medicine 47(5): 543-547.

Oleshansky, M.A., Zoltick, J.M., Herman, R.H., Mougey, E.H. and Meyerhoff, J.L. (1990). Physiological and neuroendocrine responses to maximal treadmill exercise. European Journal of Physiology 59:405-410.

Oleshansky, M. A., & Meyerhoff, J. L. (1992). Acute catecholaminergic responses to mental and physical stressors in man. Stress Medicine 8, 175-179.

Oltras, C.M., Mora, F.& Vives, F. (1987). Beta-endorphin and ACTH in plasma: effects of physical and psychological stress. Life Sciences 40: 1683-1686.
Orasanu, Judith M. and Backer, Patricia. (1996). Stress and military performance. In J.E. Driskell & E. Salas (Eds.) Stress and human performance. Mahwah, New Jersey: Lawrence Erlbaum Associates, Inc.

O'Shaughnessy, D. (2000). Speech Communications: Human and Machine. IEEE Press. Piscataway, NJ.

Ratey, J. J. (2002). A user's guide to the brain: perception, attention, and the four theaters of the brain. New York. Random House Inc.

Rosenman, R.H. (1990). Type A behavior: a personal overview. J. Soc. Behav. Pers. 5, 1-24.
Salas, Eduardo, Driskell, James E. and Hughes, Sarah. (1996). Introduction: The study of stress and human performance. In J.E. Driskell & E. Salas (Eds.) Stress and human performance. Mahwah, New Jersey: Lawrence Erlbaum Associates, Inc.

Salas, E., & Driskell, J. E. (1996). Stress and human performance. Lawrence Erlbaum Associates, Inc.
Selye, Hans (1936, 1978). The stress of life. New York: McGraw-Hill Companies.

Schedlowski, M., Weichert, D., Wagner, T. and Tewes, U. (1992). Acute psychological stress increases plasma levels of cortisol, Prolactin and TSH. Life Sciences. 50:1201-1205.

Sherwood, A. & Turner, J.R. (1992). A conceptual and methodological overview of cardiovascular research. In: Turner, J.R., Sherwood, A., Light, K.C., (Eds.) Individual Differences in Cardiovascular Response to Stress pp. 3-32.. New York: Plenum Press.

Siddle, B. K. (1995). Sharpening the warrior's edge. Millstadt, Il: PPCT Research Publications.

Spielberger, C. D., Jacobs, G. Russell, S., & Crane, R. (1983). Assessment of anger, the State-Trait Anger Scale. In J.N. Butcher and C.D. Spielberger (Eds.) Advances in personality assessment (Vol. 2, pp. 159-187). Hillsdale, NJ: Lawrence Erlbaum Associates.

Spielberger, C. D., Reheiser, E.C., and Sydeman, S.J. (1995). Measuring the experience, expression, and control of anger. In H. Kassinove (Ed.) Anger disorders: definitions, diagnosis, and treatment. Washington, D.C.: Taylor & Francis.

Spielberger, C. D., Ritterband, L. M., Sydeman, S.J., Reheiser, E.C., and Unger, K.K. (1995). Assessment of emotional states and personality traits: measuring psychological vital signs. In J.N. Butcher (Ed.) <u>Clinical personality assessment: practical approaches</u>. New York: Oxford University Press.

Spielberger, C. D., Sydeman, S.J., Owen, A.E., and Marsh, B.J. (1999). Measuring anxiety and anger with the State-Trait Anxiety Inventory (STAI) and the State-Trait Expression Inventory (STAXI). In M.E. Maruish (Ed.) <u>The use of psychological testing for traatment planning an outcomes assessment (2<u>nd</u> ed.)</u> Mahwah: Lawrence Erlbaum Associates.

Thackery, R. I., & Touchstone, R. M. (1983). Rate of initial recovery and subsequent radar monitoring performance following a simulated emergency involving startle. Federal Aviation Administration Office of Aviation Medicine; Washington, D.C.

VanDercar, D. H., Greaner, J., Hibler, N. S., Spielberger, C. D., & Block, S. (1980). A description and analysis of the operation and validity of the psychological stress evaluator. <u>Journal of Forensic Sciences 25</u>, 174-188.

Violanti, J.M., Aron, F. (1993). Sources of police stressors, job attitudes, and psychological distress. <u>Psychol Rep 72</u>(Pt 3) 899-904.

Williams, R. (1989). <u>The trusting heart: great news about type a behavior</u>. New York: Times Books.

Williams, Jr., R.B., Lane, J.D., Kuhn, C.M., Melosh, W., White, A.D. and Schanberg, S.M. (1982). Type A behavior and elevated physiological and neuroendocrine responses to cognitive tasks. <u>Science</u> 218: 483-485.

Williams, C. and Stevens, K. (1972). Emotions and speech: sine acoustical correlates. <u>J. Acoustical Soc. Amer. 52</u>(4):1238-1250.

Wilson, E.S., & Schneider, C. (1981, May/June) The neurophysiologic pathways of distress. <u>Stress/Pain Manager Newsletter</u>. Kansas City, Mo.: S/P Management Group.

Wolf, O., Schommer, N., Hellhammer, D., McEwen, B. and Kirschbaum, C. (2001). The relationship between stress induced cortisol levels and memory differs between men and women. <u>Psychoneuroendocrinology</u> 26:711-720.

Wolf., O., Schommer, N. et al. (2002). Moderate psychosocial stress appears not to impair recall of words learned 4 weeks prior to stress exposure. <u>Stress</u> 5(1):59-64.

World Health Organization's (WHO). (1998). International Classification of Diseases (ICD). (10th ed.).

Yang, R-K., Yehuda, R., Holland, D.D., & Knott, P.J. (1997). Relationship between 3-methoxy-4-hydroxyphenylglycol and homovanillic acid in saliva and plasma of healthy volunteers. <u>Biol. Psychiatry 48</u>, 821-826.

Yerkes, R.M. and Dodson, J.D., (1908) The relation of strength of stimulus to rapidity of habit-formation. <u>J. Comp. Neur. Psychol.</u> 18:459-482.

Acknowledgements

Collaborators on this research study include:

Charles D. Spielberger, Ph.D., ABPP, Distinguished Research Professor
Emeritus Director, Center for Research in Behavioral Medicine and Health
Psychology University of South Florida, Psychology Department, PCD
4118G
4202 East Fowler Avenue,Tampa, FL 33620-7200
Terry Wollert, Ph.D.
Federal Law Enforcement Training
Center Bldg. 2400
Glynco, GA 31524

James L. Meyerhoff, M.D., George A. Saviolakis, M.D., Ph.D., Bob
Burge Division of Neuroscience
Walter Reed Army Institute of Research
503 Robert Grant Ave
Silver Spring, MD 20910

Participating Investigators-Instructors / Data Collection / Task Scoring:
Jack Rinnier, Senior Instructor, Firearms Division
Darrell Walker, Detailed Instructor, ATF/Firearms Division
Steve Whittenberg, Instructor, Firearms Division
Joe Pica, Senior Instructor, Driver and Marine Division
Mike Poillucci, Detailed Instructor, USCP/Security Specialties Division
Tonya Lopez, Senior Training Research Analyst, Research & Evaluation
Division

This research was supported by the FLETC and USAMRMC.

Volunteers participated in this research only after having given their free and informed consent. Investigators
adhered to AR 70-25 and USAMRDC Reg 70-50 on the use of volunteers in research.

The views of the author(s) do not purport to reflect the position of the Department of the Army or the
Department of Defense, (para 4-3, AR 360-5).